DEBT
CONTROL

by
Chris J. Richards

Emerald Ink Publishing
7141 Office City Drive
Suite 220
Houston, Texas 77087

(713) 643-9945
Fax (713) 643-1986
E-mail emerald@emeraldink.com
http://www.emeraldink.com

Printed and bound in the United States of America

Library of Congress Cataloging-in-Publication Data

Richards, Chris J., 1962-
    Debt Control / by Chris Richards

ISBN 1-885373-19-8

Edited by Christopher Carson and Patrick Zale

Dedication

I dedicate this book to all the consumers that disclosed to me their personal finances. My heart especially goes out to my friends that found emotional support in me by my kind attitude, in helping them getting tough when dealing with their debts.

If I had to thank everybody that help me in completing this book, it would be a mess, leaving names out and including names of people who did not want their names disclosed.

Most of the consumers who helped me complete the book want to keep their personal finances personal. Thank you for finding enough trust in me to disclose your personal finances.

Most of the information I received for this book cost me money and thousands of hours of time. Some of the sources for this effort are my dear friends and neighbors. Most of these professionals I met through the Harley owners' group, but I also met hundreds of people from all walks of life. My goddaughter's father is an attorney. I love you, Caitlin.

About the Author

The author has helped consumers with their personal finances for over 15 years. Now he is going to help you with your debt management, in "Debt Control."

As a child, he lived in one of the roughest neighborhoods in Houston. In those neighborhoods, many end up in jail or dead. Here are some of his own words describing his early childhood:

> "Then I though the worst thing that could happen to me was happening: I had to share a room with my sister. I did not realize that not having a phone, air conditioning or my mother not driving a car was not the norm. My mother was my salvation during those times. That is why I am here today. She died before I grew up. Besides living with three different families and for a short time living by myself when I was fifteen years old, I was generally just as happy then as I am now. But there were times that I was not as happy, the times when I was overburdened with debt. That is why I wrote this book."

> "I started my first business when I was in high school. After graduating from high school, I thought I was too broke to go to college. I have been a top stock picker, Registered Trading Adviser, General Partner of an Investment Fund and a real estate investor."

He purchased homes, financed them himself and then sold the paper. He went through reorganization when he was overburdened with debt. Now, he is debt-free.

Today, he lives in an exclusive neighborhood. Here is what he says about what he knows about the subject of debt control:

"At thirty-five years old I am living alone. I know two things for sure: I will die and I will die debt-free."

Table of Contents

Freedom Of Choice!
I Love Being An American!

My name is Chris Richards. I love freedom of choice, and I love being an American! Today, my most important goal is to help you take care of yourself financially.

I believe a person needs to be mentally, physically and financially fit. We are all individuals: what is right for you is not necessarily right for someone else. This is true for financial fitness as well. For example, to be mentally fit, you might find therapy by going to church while someone else might find therapy by reading self-help guidelines. For physical fitness, you might walk one mile in the evening, while someone else might run five miles in the afternoon and find it more appropriate. Financial fitness will be different for you than for others, but we all need to follow the same general practices.

Just like individuals, creditors have independent requirements, too.

In this book, you will learn about the different areas of credit. Credit is a way of taking care of yourself financially. For many Americans this is a boring subject. Most people never took the time to educate themselves about credit. Most books on personal finances have only a few pages about debt. In all your years of school, how much time did you spend on learning about debt?

Why is debt an important subject? More than 80% of the average American worker's income goes to some form of debt payment. It is a staggering amount of debt. Do you know what percent of your earnings go to debt payments?

You will find out. Reading this book is an effortless way to be educated on this subject. It can save you money that you are already spending right now. In some cases, this publication can save you thousands of dollars. Some techniques have been practiced on consumers just like you, though until now, these techniques have never been revealed.

How and why should you obtain a credit report? Whether you use credit or not, you should obtain a credit report periodically to monitor the information going into your file because errors will creep in. Do you know how to dispute inaccurate information on your credit report? How to acquire lower interest rates on your credit cards? How about techniques used to eliminate finance charges on credit cards and retain a good credit report?

Do you know why state-exempt property is important to every consuming American? If you are somewhat overextended but still have good credit and want to get it under control, this book will inform you of the options available. You will learn the legal and illegal strategies credit clinics use and the pros and cons of their techniques. You will find the right direction if you are overextended or beyond recovery. If you have been turned down for a mortgage because your debt-to-income-ratio is too high, or your credit was not satisfactory, you can still do something about it. You will learn how to purchase a home, obtain the financing and protect your interest in the home.

You will read about techniques used to obtain a credit card and car, no matter how bad your credit file looks. You will learn how to put the ball in your court when dealing with creditors or collectors. You will find out if debt consolidation or a debt management program could work for you. You will learn how to get the most out of bankruptcy. Consumers can reduce their debt by 80% to 90% without filing bankruptcy, and you will soon know how!

Debt is an *expensive* topic. This publication concentrates on where the fat is, or what I refer to as *saturated fat*.

I will show you how to get *out* of debt and ways to *stay* out of debt. Here are three reasons why you should read this presentation, no matter what your debt load is.

- Expect the best in life but be prepared for the worst, because no one knows what the future holds.

- Some of the ideas in this book can be beneficial to you, even if you do not use credit.

- You do whatever you have to do—as long as it is within the limit of the law—to take care of yourself financially.

Reasons for Debt

What are the reasons for excessive debt? Usually tragic circumstances like divorce, layoff, cut in earnings, unemployment or a chronic illness in the family cause a debting problem. Other consumers accumulated a large debt load over several years by trying to provide a better life-style for the family or self. Some individuals accumulate debt due to excessive spending habits. Whatever your reason, you did not buy this publication for therapy on someone else's debt—you did it because *you* need help.

Only you can stop incurring more debt if you have a problem caused by shopping, gambling or any other out-of-control spending habit. You have to be honest with yourself and consult with the person you should take the best care of the person you see every time you stand in front of the mirror. Every gratified human knows that you must take care of yourself first.

Self-Help Groups

For people with emotional problems tied to debt, *Debtors Anonymous* offers help with group meetings nationwide. If you have emotional problems with debt, consider Debtors Anonymous. You can use your white pages to find the one near you. If you cannot find a Debtors Anonymous group near you, call 212-

642-8220 or write Debtors Anonymous, P. O. Box 400, New York, NY 10163-0400.

Our standard of living in America results from credit availability on purchases we make. If the lenders halted consumer credit, financial disaster worldwide would occur.

You do not have to accumulate debt to live a prosperous lifestyle.

Being patient will pay off in a significant way.

Where to Put the Money

Where you put your money is important. You can put your money in the right place or you can put it in the wrong place. I call it *buying protein or buying fat*. We have a choice how we spend our limited source of earnings. We can spend our money on protein items that are classified as capital assets like a house, savings plan, quality stocks, bonds and other value items or we can spend our money on fat items like expensive clothes, high-priced cars and high-ticket items that depreciate rapidly. Most of the fat items we purchase are worth less than half of the original purchase price was the day we bought the fat.

You Have A Choice

Guess what? If you're debt-free, you have a choice. You can purchase all the fat items you can afford, as long as you pay cash for the fat items.

Burdened With Debt

If you are burdened with debt, *smile*. There isn't a better place in the world to be than in the United States of America. The laws that govern banks, credit unions, collectors, credit bureaus and other companies of this type favor the consumer. I feel the laws that govern consumers should be more in favor of the consumer. Consumers are flooded with pre-approved credit card applications and billboard advertisements. Whenever you purchase something at a department store or even some convenience stores, the creditors try to sell you their credit card. You are brought up in a consuming society. The pressure is on to charge it, go in debt, spend your earnings on debt payments until you max out, and then they will stop lending you money.

You do not have to be influenced by business wanting to sell you credit.

Types of Debt

There are generally three types of debt:

- Priority debts
- Secured debts, and
- Unsecured debts.

Priority debts are unsecured debts that come first. You are usually liable for these debts under any circumstances. They include property taxes, wages, income taxes, student loans, child support and other claims of this nature.

The second form of debt is *secured debt*. There are two types of secured debt, *purchase money security interest*, and *non-purchase money security interest*. When a creditor loans you money to purchase a specific item, the creditor has a *purchase money security interest*; that item is known as *collateral*. Examples include a car loan or home mortgage. If you are unable to pay it off, the creditor may *repossess* the collateral.

Non-purchase money security interest differs from purchase money security interest in the form of the collateral you put up. When you borrow the money, you already *own* the collateral and you use the money for another purpose.

The third form of debt is *unsecured debt*. This includes credit card debt, medical bills, personal loans or any loan that actually required just your signature and that is not a priority debt. This form of debt usually gets the most attention. Because there is no collateral on these loans, they are the easiest to negotiate or discharge. In bankruptcy, unsecured debt—including credit card debt—is referred to as *dischargeable debt.* In bankruptcy, unsecured debt can be erased or discharged. This is why unsecured debt is the easiest debt to negotiate.

 **Techniques, Facts & Theories**

There are both good loans and bad loans. I am going to use my protein and fat philosophy here as an example. A good loan or *protein loan* would be used to purchase a home. A *fat loan* would be used to purchase a new car. So how do I classify credit card debt as saturated fat?

We all know that not having some fat in our finances is hard, like our collateralized car loan. But having saturated fat in finances—forget about it and start dieting.

Not all forms of unsecured loans are "saturated fat debt." Some unsecured loans are considered protein loans. Take a female consumer who obtained an education with an unsecured student loan. This consumer is using the education to benefit herself not only in the workforce but also in her personal life. Now if this consumer were not using her education to benefit herself, then the student loan would be denigrated to a fat loan or saturated fat loan.

Student Loans

If you have defaulted on a student loan, refer to the back of the book under public documents for "A Student Loan Borrower's Guide to Defaulted Student Loans."

Questionable Credit History

If your credit history is questionable, then before turning in a loan application you might be better off mailing or handing in a copy of your credit report to the creditor you want to borrow from. This will keep the inquiry section of your credit file to a minimum if the creditor turns down your request for credit. The more inquiries, the worse your credit file looks. I know of cases where the loan applicant corresponded with the lending institution's credit department over the phone about his credit report and found out it was not even worth applying for the loan. He saved himself from having another inquiry in his credit file, and he eventually received the loan from another bank. You are still going to have to fill out a loan application before the creditor makes the final decision.

Home Equity Loans and Stable Credit History

If your personal financial situation is stable—without any saturated fat in your finances—then I can understand taking out a loan against your home equity (if you will be able to itemize and write off the interest against taxable income). A good example of this type of loan: money used to purchase an automobile. If the automobile is used as collateral, the interest cannot be written off. The automobile covers the debt against the home equity loan because there is a clear title to the automobile and it is insured. Be very careful here.

Consolidation Loans

Borrowing against your home equity to pay off saturated fat debt like credit card balances can be a no-no.

To control debt and have money, do not acquire any more saturated fat in your finances.

Hint: Before you take out a loan to pay off your credit card balances, see how long you can go without charging any more purchases. A lot of consumers take out a consolidation loan to pay off their credit card balances, but then start using their credit cards. The debt only worsens by running up additional balances on the credit cards again. The debt doubles the monthly expenses because now both the new credit card payments and the consolidation loan payments must be paid. Be careful when taking out consolidation loans to pay off credit card debt.

Income Tax Withholding

Some consumers have reduced their federal income tax withholding in order to meet credit card payments or other *dischargeable debts*. Then consumers like this end up with federal income tax bills on April 15th that they cannot afford to pay. This is a major mistake. The *Internal Revenue Service* is the King of all creditors. Exempt property is not protected from the Internal Revenue Service.

Do not let a creditor or collector talk you out of money you need to pay your federal income taxes.

Rent To Own

I had a consumer ask me about rent-to-own. I told the consumer, "Do not even consider it. Rent-to-own should be outlawed. You will pay two hundred to four hundred percent more than the realistic retail price. Some loan sharks charge less in interest than rent-to-own outfits. You are better off purchasing used items out of your local classified ads. Your total purchase price on the used item you purchased out of the classified ads would equal two months installment on the rent-to-own item. Most of the time the rent-to-own item is used; they just clean it up. Stay away from rent-to-own outfits and loan sharks."

Save Auto Dollars With Assurance

Whether you have excellent or bad credit, save some major bucks and have peace of mind at the same time when you buy an automobile. You should buy a used car that is one to three years old with low miles from an individual. The car has lost the majority of its fast depreciation. Make sure the car is still under the manufacturer's warranty. If the car is still under the manufacturer's warranty, you should be able to buy the extended warranty. Do not take anything for granted. Write down the mileage and vehicle identification number, call the manufacturer to make sure you can buy the extended warranty. If you have bad credit, follow one of the techniques I explain in Chapter Four for the financing.

Credit Card Interest Rate

There is no reason why you should be paying a high interest rate on your current credit card balances if you have a good payment history. The lower the risk, the lower your interest rate.

You can often lower your interest rate by making a simple phone call to the bank that issued you your credit card. Ask for the lowest interest rate possible. Tell the bank that you have received promotional interests rates that are considerably lower than your current interest rate. You know of cases where they lowered the interest rate for other customers and you want the lowest interest rate possible. (I am sure you have received promotional applications in the mail offering lower interest rates and, more than likely, other customers at your bank are receiving lower interest rates than you are.)

The first account representative you speak to on the phone usually does not have the authority to lower your interest rate. You will have to speak to a manager or someone with authority at the bank. Be persistent about obtaining a lower interest rate and friendly. I have seen banks lower the interest rate on future and past purchases. Rarely do they lower the interest rate on cash advances. I know of consumers who literally saved hundreds to thousands of dollars a year in interest over the life of their credit card balances using this simple technique. You cannot find another investment with this kind of return for spending just a few minutes on the phone and this investment return does not cost you a dime. Nothing at all will show on your credit file for this perk.

If you have already negotiated lower interest rates in the past on your current credit card, call the creditor back and try to negotiate an even lower interest rate. You do not have to be carrying a balance in order to have your finance charges reduced, but one day you might be carrying a balance on your current credit card. When I refer to banks, I am referring to any creditor that issued you your credit card. If you have been a good-paying customer for a long time, read Chapter Eight, Get Tough With Plastic.

You may receive a promotional invitation in the mail from a bank trying to sell you their credit card at a low interest rate. If you have a good credit record and your current credit card issuing bank will not match this promotional interest rate, take full advantage of this offer. If your current credit card issuer will not match the promotional interest rate, transfer the balance to the new credit card. Sometimes the promotional initial interest rate is as low as 4.9%, and usually lasts for 6 months. After the promotional rate is over, you will likely receive another promotional invitation. You can always transfer your balances to the next bank.

You have to stay on the credit bureaus' promotional mailing list unless you can work out a reasonably low interest rate permanently with your current credit card-issuer.

Debit Cards

Many consumers find that a debit card is an excellent alternative to a credit card. This is not about your ATM debit card. It is about the ones that say Visa or Master Card on the front. You can receive the benefits of a credit card without worry about going into debt. A debting card will not let you go over your limit; it can help you break the spending habit. Call your bank to see if they offer a Visa or Master Card debit card.

If they do not offer one, find a bank that will in your Yellow Pages. Major banks used to require credit approval in order to obtain a debit Visa or Master Card, sometimes referred to as a check card. Today, morstmajor banks require only that you have a positive balance in your checking account and no credit approval.

At one time, almost all banks were reluctant to issue Visa or Master Card debit cards because they made enormous profits off of their credit cards. Now major banks realize that a debit card or check card is cheaper to process than a check. As America comes closer to being a cashless society, every consuming American should be able to obtain a plastic card that says Visa or Master Card on it. In some situations, you will need a plastic card that says Visa or Master Card. I personally got so used to using my debit card years ago that I have two of them now and only one credit card. I might be starting a new trend. Maybe one day consumers will carry a wallet full of debit cards instead of credit cards.

Car Rentals and Debit Card Worthiness

A controversial issue now rages within the realm of big business. What I am about to explain to you might not mean much to consumers that do not want to use a Visa or MC debit cards. It is very important for me because I should explain areas where I feel big businesses shortchange consumers.

If we do not try to do something about it, then nothing will change. I know from experience that if we do something about it, in our great country it can change.

Hertz and Avis car rental companies have stopped accepting Visa and MasterCard debit cards. They argue that the risk of a car leaving the lot in the hands of less-than-creditworthy customer is too great.

They also *hold* the *deposit* they initially charge your account. When you return the car, they charge your account for the rental fee on top of the deposit. Why don't they just add or subtract the balance from your initial deposit? I can understand the risk factor, but the worry over the non-creditworthy customer and deposit excuses are cheap excuses. They are not the only reasons they will not rent to what they call 'debit card customers.' The insurance that Hertz and Avis try to sell customers is unnecessary for most (who already have personal auto insurance). They still sell the insurance to the customer anyway.

Hertz and Avis should rent their cars based on the individual's appropriate insurance to cover their rental car, not on whether they have credit cards. If they require consumers to have the appropriate insurance, then Hertz and Avis should not charge these consumers for unnecessary insurance.

Is there another reason why they do not accept debt cards? Yes. Hertz is owned by Ford Motor. Millions of credit cards say Ford on them. Ford—just like the banks—makes big money off credit card loans, but Ford is not a bank. Ford will not make money off debit cards or check cards in the same way that the banks will. The remedy: use another rental car company.

Lost Debit Cards

If you lose your Visa or MC debit card, you are responsible for the first $50 as long as you report it lost within two days. What happens if over a week has passed before you realize you lost your Visa or MC debit card and your checking account is now empty? In every case I am familiar with, the banks have covered the total loss including the fifty dollars. Your debit card is tied to your checking account; it is like writing a hot check. The banks have to be careful because of the crooks. You should keep an eye on your plastic, just like you do your hair (that's a joke on a serious subject). Now, when was the last time you lost your drivers license?

Credit Card Fraud

The more credit cards you have, the higher your odds of being a credit card fraud victim. The more credit cards you have, the more exposure you have. For example, even though the creditor mails the monthly statement to you and it runs through the postal service, you might not realize that you didn't receive one of the statements. Thieves can use your credit cards for more than charging unauthorized purchases. Do not lose twenty credit cards or you might be on the phone for two days. Besides, retailers who promote their own credit cards will still take Visa or MC. Keep your plastic to a minimum.

Collector Harassment

This technique is an excellent technique to use when anyone is threatening or harassing you over the phone, such as collectors. Federal law permits you to record a phone conversation if both parties know that the phone call is being recorded. You can purchase a device that connects to your phone jack from Radio Shack or most electronic parts stores for approximately ten dollars. The device connects to any tape recorder. For another dollar, you can purchase a 'one into two prong' outlet that plugs into your phone jack. An inexpensive tape recorder costs approximately twenty dollars. For thirty-five dollars total, you could have some excellent evidence against an individual if you wanted to build a case against the collector, or it could just stop the collector from harassing you.

You must state to the individual before or right after you flip the switch on the recording phone device that this conversation is being recorded. This gives them their legal right—the option to hang up. If you use this technique in a situation with someone you know personally, be careful how you handle it, especially if you have recorded evidence. The individual could be volatile.

Check with your local telephone company on state and local laws when recording telephone conversations. I personally use this recording device as an information source, a device to help me remember.[1] Label the cassettes so you can find them if necessary and keep them organized. I recently started using my computer to store the recorded information. It is definitely preferable to having many cassettes, but it eats up my hard drive space.

---

1. I record important phone conversations. This way I can go back and use the recorded information.

For more information on this subject, refer to the back of the book under Public Documents for the Federal law on Recording Telephone Conversations.

Submitting Loan Applications

Before you submit a loan application to a mortgage company to purchase a house or apply for a loan this significant, obtain all three copies of your credit reports to make sure there are no errors or unremembered accounts.

The following example occurs frequently and causes many problems with individual loan applications. The consumer, unaware of a collection account for six hundred dollars in the credit file, still obtained credit for automobiles and other personal loans the entire time this negative mark was in the credit file.

If most of your credit is in good shape, some creditors will overlook one small collection account. In our example, she claimed that this was not *her* collection account. Whether it was her collection account or not is not the point. If she had obtained copies of her credit reports before applying for a standard mortgage, then disputed the information, or if she had followed the techniques I explain in the legal techniques of credit clinics, she could have saved time, embarrassment and money. After she settled the collection account for six hundred dollars, the mortgage company approved the loan.

The same mortgage company approved a loan for a consumer who had filed bankruptcy two years earlier. This consumer did not have any collection accounts in his credit file. Mortgage companies usually require consumers to pay off collection accounts before obtaining a mortgage.

Before applying for a major loan (or insurance or employment purposes), review your credit file. Creditors concentrate on the last two years of your credit history.

Authority

When you call a lending institution or any business, always ask to speak to someone with authority to answer your questions. Someone contacting a mortgage company will first encounter the receptionist or secretary who answers the phone. Although she feels like she is knowledgeable and wants to help, she may be misleading you. You should talk to a mortgage loan officer. When you have technical questions, always speak to someone with authority. This applies to any type of business, not just the businesses I refer to in this publication. If you feel that you did not obtain the correct information or if you want to verify the original information, you can always call back.

Newlyweds

The best advice I can give to newlyweds is to avoid credit card debt. Not using credit card debt at all would be preferable. Form a good habit of paying off your credit cards monthly. Use a debit card. Consider not even getting a credit card.

I did not realize how much of an impact credit card debt had on marriages. Credit card loans were introduced in the mid 60's and since then, the divorce rate has tripled. Credit card debt definitely increases the divorce rate and the bankruptcy cases.

Credit card debt can be as risky to your personal finances as gambling, except that credit card debt is not controlled like gambling. The creditors do not inform consumers on credit card application that charging purchases could be risky and detrimental to the future of their personal finances. There is no disclaimer.

Build Your Own Credit File

Non-traditional methods of building your own credit file can be used so that the credit bureaus will not even see them. For example, if an individual owner-financed an automobile or boat for you, you must be able to prove that you paid as agreed. Proof would be in the form of canceled checks or money orders. No law requires creditors to use your *credit report* for loan approval. The traditional use of a credit report simply makes it easier for the creditor and consumer.

Retain your own credit references using your light bill, cellular phone and other utilities as a credit reference. If you pay on time and retain your canceled checks and utility stubs, you are building proof on your credit references. Some creditors will use this as a source for credit worthiness. The only time utility companies report you to the credit bureaus is when your account is seriously delinquent.

Credit bureaus do not retain records of rent or lease payments, so keep records of your rent or lease payments. When you apply for a home mortgage, you will have to show the mortgage company your twelve to twenty-four month payment history to your landlord.

Keep Records

Remember, anytime you fill out a loan application, write a letter, statement, a dispute or any other written correspondence, make a copy to retain for your records. When it comes time to fill out another application for a loan or employment, you will remember what you wrote on the last application. I personally make copies of everything that I send out—from personal letters to financial documents. Keep your records organized and file everything accordingly. Have a box or file cabinet and retain your records in alphabetical order.

Whatever you're going to do, study it before you do it— before you fill out a loan application, before you purchase something, before restructuring your debt or whatever you decide to do. You do not have to master it but learn enough about it to feel comfortable.

Remember this quote, "Learn before you launch."

True Debt

When consumers think of debt, they include their *total debt load*. True debt is actually debt for unsecured loans, loans that are not secured by collateral. For example, take an automobile that is worth ten thousand dollars and you owe ten thousand dollars on it. If you sell the collateral, you pay off the loan and you are not in debt. A mortgage is a *collateralized loan*. If the home is foreclosed on or if you sell the home and pay off the mortgage, you are not in debt. All unsecured debt is true debt because it is not tied to any collateral and most of the unsecured debt in America is "saturated fat debt."

Credit card debt is the worst form of unsecured debt.

Each credit card you have is like taking out a loan without knowing what your total cost will be and how much your monthly payment will be. When you apply for a secured loan, you know what your total cost of the loan will be and how much your monthly payments are going to cost you.

Bankruptcy

Not only do the unemployed file bankruptcy, so also do doctors, janitors, executives, secretaries (and the list goes on). One in every seventy-five households filed bankruptcy in 1997. For a second year in a row, there will be more bankruptcy cases filed than divorces. The number one reason consumers file bankruptcy is plastic debt. Several million Americans are in some type of debt management program. We owe 1.2 trillion dollars in consumer debt. More than four hundred and fifty billion dollars of consumer debt is plastic (compared to three hundred and seventy billion in auto loans). The remaining consumer debt includes boats, trailers, student loans, mobile homes and vacations.

Savings Plans on the Job, Exempt Property?

Your 401k, IRA, pension or retirement plan can be your most treasured piece of property. If you're earning an income, you should take full advantage of an individual retirement plan. You can defer your income and earnings, and your retirement plan is generally exempt property.

Looking under your state exemptions is not enough. Consumers being sued and debtors filing their own bankruptcies have made mistakes by relying on books and software. Consumers have ended up losing a portion or their entire retirement plan, thinking it was exempt when it was not. If you are not sure if your retirement plan is exempt property, you need to consult with an attorney in your state. Call your plan administrator to find out if your retirement plan is protected by the federal law ERISA. Even if you are not allowed the federal exemptions, or if your state does not list your retirement plan as exempt property and it is protected under the federal law ERISA, it can still be exempt property. Exempt property, remember, is protected from creditors and lawsuits. Therefore, you need to make sure your retirement plan is exempt property (not all retirement plans are).

Exempt property is property you are allowed to keep if a creditor, business or individual obtains a judgment against you by favor of a lawsuit, or property you are allowed to keep if you file bankruptcy. This property is known as your state exemption or exempt property. Exempt property, however, is not protected from the Internal Revenue Service.

Exempt property rights are important to every consuming American. I have friends who are debt-free, with no mortgage on their home. These individuals carry large umbrella insurance policies. The odds of their filing bankruptcy is slim but because of lawsuits and other factors, these debt-free individuals understand how important their exempt property rights are.

At the time of this writing, the National Bankruptcy Review Committee has sent their proposals to Congress. Some members of Congress want to reduce your exempt property rights with the excuse that it is the good-paying customer who will receive reduced interest rates from the banks.

If you have studied the facts and know the past practices of the big banks, you know that when Congress reduces your exempt property rights, that money will only add to the big banks' record profits. It will not lower interest rates for consumers. The bankruptcy laws are important to every consuming American. You need to let your Congressman know how important your exempt property is to you. The bankruptcy laws need reforming, but not at the expense of the honest consuming American.

All consuming Americans should be familiar with their exempt property. Consumers tell me that protecting property is only for the rich when a financial crisis develops. This is not true. The average consumer's total net worth can equal the value of their exempt property. The consumer might have too much net worth in non-exempt property when some of it should be in exempt property. The unexpected could happen anytime, such as loss of income, medical bills, permanent disability, lawsuits or a financial crisis of some type.

Now let's discuss what property to take money out of and what property to put the money in. In other words, sell non-exempt property and invest the money in exempt property.

If you have a lot of property and a personal financial crisis develops, you might be better off moving to another state that allows generous exemptions. I am not telling you that if your financial condition is stable to sell non-exempt property and put the money in exempt property. I want you to know what your exempt property is, and the laws that govern exempt property in your state. Consult with the appropriate public offices, bankruptcy court or attorney. Find out how to properly claim your homestead exemption and all about your exempt property rights. Remember, no one knows what the future holds. Refer to the back of the book under Exempt Property for more information.

If you have a large debt load and you're thinking about borrowing or taking money out of your retirement plan or home equity, listen closely.

Do not sell or borrow money on your exempt property to pay off debts that can be discharged or negotiated.

Dischargeable debt is negotiable debt. Do not take or borrow money out of your exempt retirement plan to pay off debts like credit cards or medical bills. You should sell or borrow on non-exempt property and in some cases put the money in exempt property. For example, you should sell or borrow on a boat and put the money in exempt property like paying off loans you took out against your retirement account, use it to pay off a home equity loan or build equity in your home. Do not use the money to pay off debt that can be discharged—your financial situation could deteriorate. You could lose thousands of dollars. This does not mean you have to file bankruptcy. If you do file bankruptcy, you do not want to make last minute buys, sales or transfers. You should protect your exempt property if you have a large unsecured debt load. Exempt property varies greatly from state to state. I strongly advise you to be familiar with exempt property and homestead exemption laws in your state.

If your state does not offer a generous enough homestead exemption, then you do not want to have any equity in your home (equity available for creditors). In some cases, you might even want to borrow against your home.

What is your home worth? Consumers often think that their house and other personal property are worth more to a creditor or the bankruptcy court than they actually are. Valuing exempt and non-exempt property in most states should be at garage-sale prices. Your home is not going to appraise to a creditor or the bankruptcy court for what a professional real estate appraiser would use for market value. The house would be valued at considerably less. That is because if your home is auctioned off, it will sell for considerably less; the auction might not be enough to cover all the loans against your home.

Be aware of something else: carrying a vacant home is expensive. Taxes, insurance, maintenance and other expenses included in maintaining a home and closing costs to sell the home all add to the costs.

If you are in doubt about your state exempt property rights, consider a visit to an experienced bankruptcy attorney. You do not have to be contemplating bankruptcy to need this advice. Nobody knows your state exempt property rights better than an experienced bankruptcy attorney in your state. Most bankruptcy attorneys will not charge you for consultation. A consultation with a bankruptcy attorney will definitely be worth the time and money if a financial crisis ever develops. Personal injury attorneys and bankruptcy attorneys make up half the Yellow Pages. You should not have a hard time finding a good bankruptcy attorney.

Moral Obligations

When I refer to creditors in this presentation, I am not referring to creditors you owe priority debts to (like the Internal Revenue Service) unless I specifically inform you.

Do not let creditors, collectors or anybody else control you emotionally.

They might say, "It is your moral obligation to pay your debts." The only thing that you are morally obligated to do is take care of yourself and your family. The creditor took the risk and lent you the money. How often have you taken risk and it did not pan out? If you're burdened with debt and you do what you should do, the worst thing that will happen to you for not paying your debts is a bad credit report. A bad credit report can be repaired.

Right To Deposits

If you have a credit card at the same bank as your checking account, you have money on deposit. The bank can take the money you have deposited if you become delinquent on your credit card account. This right to take deposits does not apply to exempt property like a retirement account (if it is exempt property in your state).

Validity of the Information and Research

I spent thousands of hours researching the material in this publication. I obtained information from the U.S. Code, FTC, FCC, consumers, friends, corporate organizations, attorneys and several other sources, including my most cherished educator, the school of experience. If I received oral information, I verified it by the rules or laws that govern the oral information I received. I received oral information from attorneys and other professionals whom I believed to be reliable. When I researched the rules or laws that governed that information, the oral information given to me by professionals was occasionally wrong. You must take care of yourself. I cannot give you any guarantees on the information or strategies presented. Rules do change. Laws change too, but not as fast as rules.

Mortgage Money & A Home For Everybody

Any consumer can use these aids when financing a home. These techniques can offer you some money saving ideas.

Applying for a Standard Mortgage

When a lending institution such as a mortgage finance company handles the financing for a home, it is called a standard mortgage. A consumer *loses* money on the purchase of a home. This statement is true for the following reasons:

1. **Finance charges**. The consumer is overcharged in finance charges (annual percentage rate or APR) because he has bad credit or the consumer with excellent credit simply paid too much for finance charges. You should always shop around for a mortgage. The poorer your credit rating, the more shopping you need to do. A half or quarter percent more added to your mortgage in finance charges can end up costing you thousands of dollars more in finance charges added to the life of the mortgage.

2. **Custom home**. The consumer wants to purchase a new or custom home.

3. **Sale of home**. The consumer sells his existing house a lot sooner than expected and purchases another home. The average American sells his house approximately every five years. Usually the consumer is not even thinking about selling, but is set on buying the home. Remember that you not only pay closing costs when you purchase a home, you

also pay closing costs when you sell the same home. For every two homes you purchase you're paying closing costs four times. Closing costs on a new mortgage are expensive. Costs include contracts, real estate agent fees, points, title insurance, and other expenses.

4. **First offer**. The buyer offers too much money to the seller on the first offer. *The listing real estate agent is working for the seller, not the buyer*. The real estate agent wants to close the deal, to get paid. Do not forget that real estate agents work on commissions only. I have purchased several homes. When I made my first offer, the agent working for me said it was a ridiculously low offer for the home and she was too embarrassed to make the proposal. However, I ended up paying a ridiculously low price for the home.

5. **Time on the market**. The longer the home has been on the market, the lower your offer should be. Usually the buyer of another home is more desperate to sell the old home. Find out how long the home has been on the market. I promise you if you do not purchase the first home you try to buy with a low offer, you will find another one you like just as much.

6. **Location of the home**. The home is purchased in a depressed or declining area. Even if the home is in a newly developed community, you could be purchasing a money pit. Drive around the neighborhood and look at how many 'For Sale' signs are posted. I am not telling you not to buy a home because the neighborhood has too many 'For Sale' signs or it is a new master planned community that can be duplicated. You may have sound reasons to buy in this area. You may have children and this new master planned community offers excellent public education. Your children's well being is more important than making or saving money on a home. If the neighborhood has a large percentage of 'For Sale' signs, then there are more desperate

sellers to be found in the neighborhood. You could possibly find a bargain from a very desperate seller willing to negotiate on price or terms.

7. **Bad credit file.** Purchasing a home now might end up costing you a lot more because of your personal financial situation. You might have a bad credit file. Consider taking care of your finances and purchasing a home that will cost you less or one that you can actually make some money on.

Credit Ratings

A consumer with good credit or "A" credit will receive the standard interest rate, or the same interest rate as someone with perfect credit. Good credit applies to automobile loans as well as mortgages.

What is good credit? Consumers with a good credit history or "A" credit will qualify for a loan with the lowest interest rate offered by the lender. Good credit does not mean you have a perfect credit history. If creditors could only make loans to consumers with a perfect credit history, they would not be able to make enough loans to stay in business. You have to be able to prove you have a good credit history, either through a credit report or through nontraditional means such as your own credit file.

A good credit rating will be based on several factors. The first is mortgage or rent payments. Some lenders go back only twelve months. The majority of the creditors go back twenty-four months. You should not have any late mortgage or rent payments in the past twenty-four months. Good past mortgage or rent payments equal GOOD CREDIT.

The second factor emerges from automobile or other secured loan payments. Most creditors consider your payment history on automobile loans as important as your rent or mortgage. You should not have any late auto payments in the past twenty-four months. On-time auto payments equal GOOD CREDIT.

Late payments do not mean paying before the due date. Late payments mean the creditor received your payment before it is considered late. Look on your statement or in your lease agreement. It will tell you when your payment is late. Mortgage payments are usually considered late 15 days after the due date. Usually you are reported late to the credit bureaus 30 days after the due date.

Credit Cards or unsecured loans generate good credit ratings. When it comes to credit card loans, creditors are much more forgiving. If you were 30 days late on making two of these payments, but not over 60 days late on any credit card or unsecured loan in the past twelve months, this equals GOOD CREDIT.

If you have no outstanding debts such as collection accounts, charge-offs or judgments, you will likely have GOOD CREDIT. Some creditors will overlook a collection account if you have a good excuse and evidence to go along with the excuse. The statute of limitations can be a factor when dealing with collection accounts and charge-offs. Creditors can be understanding about medical collection accounts but judgements are usually an automatic loan turn down.

As long as your income is sufficient to service your monthly payments and you have *four* "GOOD CREDITS," then you are usually in the door for a standard mortgage—the front door of your new home. If you have bad credit, read Chapter Four on rebuilding your credit.

You may have good credit even with a bankruptcy in your credit file. You must have a good reason why you filed bankruptcy. At least two years have passed since your bankruptcy was discharged. You have established at least three lines of credit since your discharge. You do not have any late payments whatsoever. You must have PERFECT CREDIT since your bankruptcy discharge.

After you have obtained all three copies of your credit report and you feel your credit history is questionable, set an appointment with a mortgage broker to review your credit reports.

Nobody knows the mortgage business better than a qualified mortgage broker. You might want to consult with more than one mortgage broker to obtain different opinions. Use your local Yellow Pages to find a mortgage broker. Using a mortgage broker to review your credit files is like having a free credit analysis. *Some consumers pay hundreds of dollars to a credit clinic for the same service.* When meeting with a mortgage broker, bring up other factors like job stability and sufficient income to qualify for a mortgage. When applying for a standard mortgage, "usually" the mortgage company requires that your total monthly debt payments, including the mortgage, not be more than 38% of your gross income.

If you have the money and income, you can obtain a mortgage even with a bad credit file. The mortgage business is very competitive. Look in your Yellow Pages under mortgage companies, or in large metropolitan Sunday newspapers or on the Internet, and you will see advertisements offering mortgages to consumers with bankruptcy, foreclosure, charge-offs or other derogatory information. With bad credit, you might have to pay extra for a mortgage. Do not pay any more than you have to. Just as no two bankruptcies are alike, no two mortgage applicants are alike. For example, the mortgage company will determine interest rates by time since discharge from bankruptcy and credit history since discharge. After a bankruptcy discharge, you can have an A credit rating within two years.

If your credit report has negative information and you want to qualify for a mortgage, you could be better off using *patience*. Patience can save you tens of thousands of dollars in finance charges. Call a mortgage company and ask questions that pertain to your personal situation.

Remember, you can always move to the next house. Never be desperate or you can lose control. Desperation can be expensive. There are too many homes for sale.

Financing With Very Bad Credit

How did two consumers with very bad credit files finance their homes with standard mortgages?

They used mommy and daddy. Parents apply for the mortgage and get approval. The homeowner's insurance is in the name of the kid, or consumer with a bad credit file. Homeowners insurance is not in the parents name. One of the two kids wanted to protect his legal interest in the home because of the heirs to his parents estate. He had his parents sign over a *quitclaim deed*. He filed the quitclaim deed through the public records office. His parents did not care about the mortgage being reported in their credit file as a monthly expense.

What if his parents wanted to apply for a loan and needed evidence that they were not financially obligated for his mortgage? He could draw up a lease agreement for his parents to use as evidence to show the creditors his parents were not financially obligated. In a family situation like this, bank account statements and canceled checks are good evidence to show who is financially obligated for the mortgage. As long as his parents proved that they were not financially obligated for the mortgage, the monthly mortgage payment would not go against his parents income when they applied for a loan.

A *quitclaim deed* is a legal instrument used to grant whatever title the grantor has, if the grantor has any title. Here his parents were granting over their ownership. There are several types of deeds, used for different purposes. In most states, quitclaim deeds are usually used between spouses.

A Home For Everybody!

This chapter applies to everyone because you can *make* money following these techniques without using a lot of money. The techniques were designed for consumers who are unable to qualify for a mortgage because their credit ratings are insufficient, their incomes are too low, they have high debt-to-income ratio or they are unable to make the required down payment.

As a matter of interest, I have used and been on both sides of these following contracts. I have never encountered any legal problems with them. If I purchased the property without searching for liens, I would have encountered legal problems.

Lease Option To Purchase Agreement. Lease option to purchase agreement is a contract that grants the right to use the real estate for a period of time with an option to purchase before the lease expires.

Contract for deed. Contract for deed is a method of selling and financing real estate. The buyer takes possession of the home while making payments to the seller. The seller holds legal title until the contract is paid off or converted to a deed of trust. Contract for deed is also referred to as a *land contract* or *installment contract*.

A **wraparound mortgage** wraps around any existing mortgage and is junior to any other mortgage tied to the real estate. The advantage of a wraparound mortgage: you can purchase title insurance. The disadvantage: the wraparound concept may not work when the mortgage debt to be wrapped contains an *alienation clause*. An alienation clause or *due-on-sale clause* gives the lender the right to call the entire balance due if the mortgaged property is sold by the borrower. In other words, the wraparound mortgage is not always possible because you are telling the lender the property is sold. If a wraparound mortgage is not possible, you can use a contract for deed. I have never seen a mortgage company call a mortgage due on a lease-to-purchase option or a contract-for-deed sale. If you call the lender up on the phone and tell them, "I have a contract for deed tied to your mortgage," they might hang up on you or call the mortgage due. As long as the original lender is getting paid as agreed, there should not be anything to worry about. When I use this type of financing, I always use a contract for deed and instruct consumers on how to use a contract for deed.

Usually after three years, the due-on-sale clause kicks in, no matter what type of contract is used. I am familiar with several contract for deeds that are more than ten years old. The lenders never ask for the mortgage to be paid off because the lender never knew the house was sold. You can register your lease with option to purchase contracts and contract for deeds through the public records office or county court house. Registering your contracts through the public records office does not mean the mortgage company is going to know about it. I will cover this at the end of the Chapter.

When using these strategies, I like finding homes that are not listed by a real estate agency. Usually dealing directly with the homeowner is beneficial to the buyer. You can close good deals occasionally with agents as well. Some real estate agents are in the business of buying, financing and selling homes.

You can find these types of homes in your newspaper classified ads and local free papers, by driving around neighborhoods that interest you, through friends or family members and from any other sources you can think of. One of my favorite ways is to run an ad in the local newspaper classified section stating any of the following different statements:

- I buy homes in need of repair.

- Looking for a lease-to-purchase option.

- Will purchase home in any condition if owner is willing to finance.

The majority of the homeowners will not pay any attention to your ad because they want to sell their house right now for cash. But one day, some of these same owners that wanted to sell their house for cash "today" will be looking for other ways to sell their home:

1. There are always those desperate sellers who have "had it" with real estate agents because of poor or no results.

2. Because their homes are harder to sell when in

need of repairs.

3. The homeowners want to sell or lease their home on their own.

4. Some homeowners are paying for a new home before selling their old home.

The homeowners who bought a new home before selling their old home represent the best candidates for a *lease with option to purchase agreement* or *contract for deed*. They were so excited about buying their new home. After they move into their new home, the excitement wears off and paying monthly payments for two mortgages starts wearing thin. These homes are usually in good condition. If you are not able to talk the owner into a contract for deed, try a lease with option to purchase agreement or move on to the next house. Do not get upset if you do not close the deal. Look at it as a learning experience that cost less money than an hour at Defensive Driving School. You should look at each learning experience as an hour credit in college that will definitely weigh in your favor on your next adventure in real estate.

You will be surprised what a simple classified ad that cost you forty dollars to run can do for you. If you run a classified ad, make sure your ad states that you are an "individual wanting to purchase a residence" or "individual wants lease with option to purchase, as a resident." This same rule applies whenever you speak to a homeowner: make sure they know that you want the home as your personal residence and you're not an investor that will rent or lease it out to someone else. Being a resident of the home you intend to purchase or lease will definitely weigh in your favor when negotiating terms. This does not mean you can never rent or sell the house to someone else. Down the road, anything is possible. You might end up selling it for a profit.

By the way, I have always avoided rental property. My philosophy is to:

• Purchase a home that needs repairs.

• Sell it by owner finance.

- Buyer repairs the house.

- I sell the note and keep the profit.

- Leave some money for the next round and spend the rest of the profits.

Mortgage companies and investment groups buy lease-with-option-to-purchase agreements and contract-for-deeds. That means that *the seller has a market to sell the contract for deed and you have a market to find a mortgage for your lease with option to purchase agreement.*

If You Cannot Get A Standard Mortgage

If the seller sells the contract for deed, she can pay off the original mortgage and get her equity out of the home.

This can be your best negotiating tool when dealing with the seller. Tell her there is a market out there to sell the contract for deed and she can pay off the original mortgage and get her money out of the home. You as the buyer must have a good payment history in order for the seller to sell the contract. It is your obligation as the buyer to pay as agreed. Of the contracts I am familiar with, usually twenty-four months pass after the property is sold before the seller sells the conrtact. This gives the contract time to mature. If you cannot get approval for a standard mortgage, you can still purchase a home and obtain financing from an outside source. Lenders usually turn the contract into a deed of trust.

A *deed of trust* is a transfer of legal title to the property from the trustor to the trustee, placing the legal title with the trustee until the mortgage is paid off. I think of a deed of trust as a standard mortgage you get when a large mortgage company finances your home. You can buy *title insurance* to guarantee your ownership in the home with a deed of trust. In other words, you are in complete control of your ownership in the home. Unlike a contract for deed, your trust is based on the person that sold you the house. Like I said earlier, I will show you how to protect your interest when using a contract that you cannot buy title insurance for. You can never be too careful.

Buying owner financed notes has become more competitive than it was in the past. Some guys buying these notes (or what I am referring to as contracts) will try to rip off the person selling the contract. It will be the owner's responsibility to shop around to sell your contract for deed, and your responsibility to shop around for financing on a lease with option to purchase agreement.

Another advantage of the contract for deed is your closing costs. Of the homes I sold and bought, the closing costs were usually one hundred dollars plus the property taxes and down payment. Sometimes I would draw up the contract for deed myself and save a hundred dollars. No appraisal, no points, no title insurance, etc. When it comes time to sell the contract, the closing costs are factored into the cost of buying the contract. That means if the seller sells your contract, the contract will be discounted in the note. You and the seller can work that out or just go with the flow. Whatever you do, make sure it weighs in your favor.

The seller should be more than willing to include the closing costs in carrying the contract or mortgage for you. The title policy is usually paid for by the seller and all other closing costs can be factored into the purchase price of the home, just like in a standard mortgage at closing.

If you're not paying for closing costs, offer the seller a more competitive price or better terms. Houses rarely sell for their asking price. Not all private homeowners are savvy investors, while most real estate agents and investors usually are. Remember, in real estate, everything is negotiable. You can always offer more, but never less.

In a contract for deed, the home purchaser, meaning you, usually has the option of turning the contract for deed into a deed of trust. That means you will be paying the closing costs. If the owner never sells your contract for deed, you might want to turn your contract for deed into a deed of trust sometime in the future.

Homes In Need Of Repair

Let's look now at homes in need of repair. You can use a contract for deed on a home in good or bad condition. When purchasing a home in need of repairs, you will want to use a contract for deed or deed of trust as the legal instrument. Do not sink money in a home on a lease with option to purchase agreement.

Since most of us are not carpenters, you might be saying, "I do not want to buy a home in need of repairs." If your credit is not satisfactory, if you do not have enough for a down payment or if you are not able to get approval for a standard mortgage because of personal reasons, this is one way to buy a home for a low down payment. Buying a home in need of repairs will not only bring you ownership in a home, it will also allow you to build equity fast or make some money. Even if you have perfect credit and you're filthy rich, you can use this technique to get richer.

Real estate agents will always pull your credit file. In some cases, an individual seller will pull your credit file. The individual seller usually relies on past employment history and references. If you are asked about your credit file because of negative information like bankruptcy or collection accounts, explain your situation. For example, if you discharged only unsecured debt in bankruptcy, but paid for all your collateralized secured loans as agreed, make sure they know this. Several of my friends, investors and I have financed many homes in need of repair and never pulled a credit report on the buyer. Your down payment is made when you repair the house. Most of these homes sell for a very low down payment, and a few for zero down.

One transaction I completed over 15 years ago. I am using this old example for two reasons: the first reason—I committed in this book to give some pointers on making money by borrowing money. The second reason—I never paid off the balances on the credit cards. I would never use a credit card like this today, but that does not mean you can't. I probably do not have anything to worry about, because after writing this book, *Debt Control*, I do not think a bank will give me another credit card. The one credit card I have will be taken away. The only thing I use the credit card for is a decoy for my goddaughters' Lhasa Apso. It has dog bites all over it.

I found my first home by running and ad in the classified section of the free paper saying, "I Pay Cash For Houses, Any Condition." Everyone else ran ads saying. "I Buy Homes." These were the investors trying to build net worth by getting everyone to finance the house for them. At that time, I was the only one that advertised cash for homes in this free paper. Now there are over twenty or thirty guys running ads in this same free paper saying, "I Pay Cash For Houses, Any Condition." This is good for you because there are more investors doing the low down no credit check deal.

I think this guy wanted out of town fast. He responded to my ad. I did all the legal stuff and bought the house. In a cash deal like this, always buy title insurance. I charged the home for $8,000. I took cash advances out on my credit cards. At 18 years of age and one dollar in the bank, I was buying a home for zero down. That same home I sold for $22,500. The down payment was $500 with owner finance 15 years. I did not have to sell the contract for deed, because in less than a year the buyer sold the house for forty thousand dollars. He put only a few thousand dollars in the home for repairs. He made over $10,000. If you use credit cards like this, pay them off and make sure you buy insurance on the home. That is what I did not do on another home. I was 19 years old and lost every dime. The banks give credit cards to teenagers like candy. I will cover this subject more in Get Tough With Plastic.

Besides running an ad in your local newspaper in the classified section, you can find these homes by looking in any local paper for 'For sale by owner.' A consumer can find out how to buy a home by looking in all the local papers, especially the free papers. Find ads that say "We pay cash for homes, any condition." You find them before they find you. Call these mortgage companies and inventors to see what homes they have available and at what terms. I still have consumers call me to see if I have any homes for sale. Please do not call me now to buy a home. You can see what I am doing right now. By the way, I type with two fingers and think with one of them.

Make a list of all the materials you will need to repair the home. Go to a building supply store with your list and add up the total cost of all the material on your list. This is added to your expense sheet. Do not worry about factoring the cost of repairing the house into the price of the home. That sounds ridiculous, but let me tell you why you shouldn't factor these costs into the cost of the home. You main goal is to pay a ridiculously low price for the home. You should be able to just look at the list and see a major difference in your return.

These homes can be found in all types of neighborhoods. The more expensive the neighborhood, the less likely you are to find a home in need of repairs. If you do not want to buy a home that is in need of repairs, or if you're not sure you want to buy this particular home, consider a lease with option to purchase agreement as the contract of choice. When you negotiate your original rent or lease option to purchase agreement, have a portion of your monthly payments go toward the purchase price of the home. If you find the right seller and negotiate a large enough portion of your monthly payment to go toward your purchase price of the home, you can build more equity in the home in the first few years than you would with a 15 or 30 year mortgage. In the first few years of a 15 or 30 year mortgage, only a small percentage of your monthly payment is going toward the principle.

With a lease option to purchase agreement, you will not be able to write off the interest because there are no finance charges. Even without the advantage of tax-deductible finance charges, it can still be more beneficial to using a lease option to purchase agreement, if you negotiate a large enough portion of your monthly payment to go toward the purchase price of the home. Even if you are only able to negotiate ten percent of the lease payments to be applied to the purchase price, it is still a start in becoming a homeowner. The IRS considers a contract for deed an installment sale. If you itemize, you can write off the interest on a contract for deed.

Lease-to-purchase contracts usually last twenty-four to sixty months before your option to purchase expires. The longer you negotiate your original lease for, the more beneficial the arrangement is to you. This will give you more time to meet the qualifications for a mortgage. You can purchase the home anytime before your original lease agreement expires. Try to lock in a purchase price on the home at the time you sign your lease-to-purchase agreement. Some owners will want to use the future market value of the house when you make the actual purchase. All the legal technicalities will be stipulated in your original lease agreement. Make sure you understand everything written in your original lease with option to purchase agreement.

When you close on the first mortgage, use the portion of your monthly payment going toward the purchase price of the home you're leasing with 'option to purchase' as part of the down payment. This will lower your closing costs when you go to closing for a standard mortgage. If you have bad credit, with a lease-to-purchase agreement you will be establishing credit and you will already be in the home you are going to purchase. Keep your monthly payment records and pay on or before the due date. Your monthly payment records will be one of the most important records that the underwriter will use when making the final decision on approving your mortgage.

If the owner rejects your first offer and you like the home enough, offer a larger deposit. This deposit will become available as cash when you close on the first mortgage. Never make offers or payments that you cannot afford. Never offer more money until your first written offer is rejected.

You can find rent or lease-to-purchase homes in your newspaper classified ads. Call the owners of houses for rent or lease only, and ask the owner if she is interested in giving you the option to purchase her property if you lease it from her. Make sure you let her know the home will be your personal residence. A disadvantage with a lease option to purchase agreement comes when it is time to apply for the mortgage and you are not approved. Make sure you are meeting the qualifications to be approved for a mortgage on the home you signed a lease-to-purchase agreement on. Do not agree to making any major repairs in your lease-to-purchase agreement. You do not want to sink any money in a home that you might not own.

Real Estate Agents as Consultants

Real estate agents work on commissions only. This means that there is no charge for information. It is like having another free consultant. No doubt you have a lot of questions that you want answered. Find a home that interests you, and call the listing agent to make friends. You do not have to tell her that you're not going to purchase this specific home; she already knows that. Real estate agents show hundreds of homes and answer thousands of questions before making a sale. Even if you're not ready to purchase, you can still set up an appointment with the listing agent to look at a home and ask questions that will educate you for future reference. The real estate agent knows even if you do not use her service to the fullest this time, next time you might use her service when you decide to sell or purchase a home.

The real estate agent wants the commission, even if the commission is not paid out immediately. Real estate agents can be paid out over time if your contract with the buyer requires you to pay the buyer out over time. For example, on an owner finance contract, the commissions can be worked out between the seller and agent or you and the agent.

Word of caution: some real estate agents are worse than a door-to-door vacuum cleaner salesmen—both work on commissions. Do not let a real estate agent talk you into making any fast financial decisions. The Internet and your public library are other excellent sources of information on real estate contracts, laws and other educational information.

Contracts

You might be saying to yourself, "I do not even know how a contract for deed looks like, much less any other real estate contract." Go get some contracts and look at them before you sign one. While you're picking up a contract for deed or lease with option to purchase agreement, make sure you pick up an *earnest money* contract, some times referred to as a purchase contract. Pick up every real estate contract you can get your hands on. You can get these contracts from an office supply store, real estate agent, Internet, software and friends. Go to a title company and ask them for blank contracts. A title company or attorney will give you blank contracts.

When it is time to draw up the contract, call several attorneys or anybody else for a price quote on preparing the contract for you. If you feel confident, you can do it yourself. Be careful. Some attorneys will overcharge you for simple contracts. Instead of an attorney, use a paralegal to do the typing. Use the Yellow Pages to find paralegals.

An earnest money contract, commonly called a purchase contract, goes along with a cash deposit to guarantee your commitment to buy the property. If you default or change your mind, the seller keeps the deposit. Keep your deposit that goes along with the purchase contract to a minimum. You might change your mind and lose your money.

Inspections

If you do not feel that you are capable of inspecting the home yourself, hire a professional inspector. You do not need a professional real estate appraisal when you're buying a home in need of repairs or lease with option to purchase agreement. A professional home inspection usually cost $150, as compared to a professional real estate appraisal costing approximately $400. A local real estate agent will be glad to give you a printout of what other homes sold for in the neighborhood. Use this printout as reference. It will have information on it you can use for comparison.

You can inspect the home yourself. Look in the attic for structural damage and termites. Walk around the house to inspect the slab. Turn on and off all the light switches and water supplies. Punch on the walls or anything else you can think of. Call an exterminator for a free termite inspection.

This is the way I protect my interest when doing a contract for deed, lease with option to purchase or any other real estate contract that does not go through a title company. It is still as effective today as it was years ago. Now I pay for a service to have access to public records information through my computer.

Liens

A lien is a claim on the property for a business or individual as security for a debt. The most common liens against a home are a judgement lien, tax lien and mechanic's lien. *A title company will not issue title insurance on a home with a lien*. Do not buy a home with a lien against it unless you know exactly what you are doing.

A judgement is like a lien, but it is against a business or individual. A judgement is the final word of the court. If you lose a lawsuit, then a judgement is placed against you until you pay off the business or individual that was awarded the lawsuit. A judgement can and will create a lien against any property owned by the individual or business that lost the lawsuit.

Title insurance is a policy issued by a title company that guarantees your ownership in the home you purchased.

Always ask for the seller's drivers licence when purchasing a home from a stranger. I have always shown my driver licence to any consumer that wanted to purchase a home from me. Make sure you get a full name and address off the licence.

Tell the owner you want to look at the last title insurance policy issued for the house. Get the legal description off the title insurance policy. To feel even better, call the title company that issued the last title insurance policy to verify that it is correct.

Now you're off to the County Court House or public records office. This is where all records that go through the courts are open to the public. Call the County Court House before you leave and tell them what you are looking for. If you live in a large metropolitan area you might be able to find an annex close by. Depending on what part of the country you live in, searching public records can be either relatively easy or a real hassle. Whatever the case, there is always a clerk to help you.

You will be looking for liens and back taxes in the county the house is in. You will receive a piece of paper from the clerk with the owner's name, tax assessed value and legal description. Hopefully, you do not find any negative information such as back taxes or liens. When I found no liens on the property, I did not check for judgments against the individual. In the majority of the states, if the seller has a judgement against him, then the property would have a lien against it. This is not always true. Different states have different laws. You can check to see if there are any judgements against the individual too.

Land Search

For a fee, you can have a title company do a land search for you. This is an extensive search. If you do a land search, you do not have to search the public records for liens. You can use the same title company as your escrow agent—they can hold your deed until you acquire your first mortgage or the seller sells the contract to deed to a mortgage company. Let the title company you use as an escrow agent know that you will use their services to purchase your title insurance. The title company should deduct the land search fee from your future title insurance costs. The seller usually pays for title insurance.

For Ladies Only

Never enter a vacant home by yourself. I have seen freaks inside these homes. When the house is vacant, these same freaks turn into super freaks.

I have explained a few ideals to you in this chapter. By educating yourself, you can create even better ideals. With a little determination, you can end up on the other side of the coin and become an investor in real estate (that is, if you want to be an investor).

I have used techniques that have not generally been revealed to the public, but have been practiced privately to purchase homes. These methods go beyond foreclosures, IRS repossessions, tax liens, HUDs and running ads in your local newspapers asking for homes. Some of these techniques are a lot less work. If you would like to know more about these, you will have to write me for my next book!

Credit Cards & Cars, Rebuild Your Credit File

How can we obtain a credit card and automobile no matter how bad our credit file looks? Here are ways to build or rebuild credit. This chapter will save you money, too!

If you think you are being overcharged on the finance charges for an automobile loan, try paying your creditors on time for two years. The last two years of your credit history are usually the most critical.

Whether you are establishing credit, have bad credit, a charge-off, collection accounts or you recently just came out of a bankruptcy, this chapter will help you.

Do not get wrapped up in an organization that is trying to sell you a loan, especially if your credit history is bad. A bad credit file tends to make a consumer too desperate. For example, the Internet and world wide web offer excellent information, but many sites try to sell you a loan package or whatever they have to offer. If you obtain a mortgage from the sponsor of a credit information source, you might pay a quarter- or half-percent interest more than you have to. This could end up costing you thousands of dollars over the life of the mortgage because you did not shop around. This goes for credit cards, auto loans and so forth.

Rebuilding Credit

It will be hard to establish or reestablish independent credit—and impossible with some creditors—if you do not have a checking account number.

The following techniques represent the cheapest ways to obtain or rebuild credit.

1. If you have a friend or family member with a certificate of deposit or savings account at a lending institution, ask them if they will put it up as collateral so you can obtain a low interest loan. To help the family member or friend feel more comfortable in putting up their savings as collateral, ask for a small loan against their certificate of deposit or savings. A one thousand dollar loan at whatever terms you can afford is a good starting point. Family members or friends are a good source. You do not want them to have to pay back whatever portion of the loan you did not pay for. One way of talking them into doing this is to give the money you borrowed from them right back to them. Right after the bank gives you the loan, you give them the money. You will not be in debt to them. After you pay off the loan, they will return your money to you. You can think of your loan payments as a savings plan and establishing credit.

2. You can put up your own money and borrow against it. The only problem with putting up your own money is that the bank might require you to have more money in your savings account or C. D. than you can afford. You can always use your Yellow Pages to call local banks; see which ones will work with you and how much money they require you to have in your savings account in order to use it as a collateral for a loan. After you pay off the loan, make sure it is reported to the credit bureaus.

3. Get easy credit but not expensive credit. Do not get a credit card from a 900 number, or a gold or platinum card that is not from a reputable source. Some of these companies will sell you their credit card that you can use only to buy their overpriced merchandise. I do not care if they offer you a $10,000 line of credit—you will

get ripped-off. When it comes to easy credit, and it sounds too good to be true, it is a rip-off.

4. Apply for easy credit from reputable creditors such as convenience stores, gas stations, auto parts, Radio Shack and other national specialty retailers. It is relatively easy to get credit approval from these types of creditors.

5. Rebuild credit with a secured credit card. Open a savings account as a security deposit at a bank that offers consumers a secured credit card. This is the most common way consumers with a bad credit file re-establish credit. If you are not careful, it can be a very expensive way to re-establish credit. More banks than ever are getting into the secured credit card business. That is good for you because it is more competitive. Competition brings lower cost to the consumer. The costs of secured credit cards have come down. Find the lowest finance charges and up-front fee possible. Do not get a secured credit card from a third party even if they promise you the moon. Always deal directly with the bank that issues the secured credit card. Do not deal with offshore banks either. Pull out your Yellow Pages and go to work. Two reputable banks that issue secured credit cards promote their secured credit cards on TV.
If you are unable to find a reputable bank that issues a secured credit card, send a self-addressed stamped envelope to Debt Control (the address is in back of the book). You will be provided with a list of national banks that are currently offering secured credit cards.

6. If you get a secured credit card to reestablish credit, do not forget to use it. Creditors will want to see how you handle your new credit, so use it wisely. Paying it off monthly is very wise.

7. Ask a family member or friend to open a joint charge card account with you. Tell them you want to start

building credit. They might feel more compelled to help you if you ask them to start you out with a low limit, like five hundred dollars. If required, let them keep the credit card and you build credit. Tell them they have to use the credit card in order for you to build credit. All joint accounts are reported on both credit files. If you have very bad credit and apply, you could be turned down—that will add an inquiry to your credit file.

8. Here is a low-cost way of obtaining a credit card. Ask a family member or good friend to allow you to be an authorized user on one of their major credit cards. They might feel more compelled to help you if you ask them to designate their lowest limit credit card or even open a new account for you with a five hundred dollar line of credit. They will receive the monthly statements and you will issue them a check each month. When you are an authorized user, you are just that—a user. You will not have any authority over the credit card. All the credit information should be reported in their credit file. If you do not pay as agreed, you will lose a friend or have a mad family member. It has been stated or written that when you become an authorized user on somebody else's credit card account, their credit history will be absorbed on your credit file. This is not always true. The two different credit files merge because of the way the credit bureaus collect information. The way they identify you is not based solely on your Social Security number. That is because so many people have similar names, live at the same address, or have other similar details. You might get lucky because the creditor has the *option* of reporting an authorized user but is not *obligated* to reporting an authorized user unless they are married. If you authorized your spouse to be a user on your individual credit card account, the creditor must report your spouse as well as your credit history associated with the authorized account to the credit bureaus.

Automobiles and Credit

When you are financing a vehicle, bad credit can cost you thousands more in finance charges. When you go shopping with a bad credit file for a vehicle, concentrate not only on the price of the vehicle but also the finance charges as well.

An automobile loan is the easiest loan to get. Most major car dealership's offer high interest loans no matter what your past credit history is, as long as you make a large enough down payment and your employment is stable. The worse your credit, the more you pay in finance charges. The more your down payment, the lower your finance charges. Car loans are among the easiest ways to reestablish new credit but they are a very expensive way. Due to the high finance charges, you end up paying thousands more than the average consumer will pay. Bad credit can cost you $1,000 to $15,000 more in finance charges.

The best advice is to shop around for finance charges and take your credit reports with you. If you take your credit reports with you when shopping around for a vehicle, you do not have to worry about the dealership asking you to sign a release to pull your credit file. Make friends with the finance manager. The finance manager has more stroke than he wants you to believe.

Make sure you tell the dealership you do not want an inquiry on your credit report unless you purchase the vehicle from them. This will also show that you care about your credit file. Many dealership's use the credit bureaus scoring system only as a guideline. If your main goal is to re-establish credit, there are other ways that will save you thousands compared to a high interest car loan. For example, a secured credit card is a lot cheaper way to reestablish credit.

When you buy a brand-new car with a bad credit file, your down payment can cost you more than paying cash for a clean used car would. The dealership might require 33% down. I would start shopping for a clean used car from an individual and reestablish credit using a secured credit card. For what your new monthly payment will be, at 32% interest you could get a secured credit card and have enough in a savings account to put up as collateral to borrow against in a few months. Three new lines of credit and you're on your way to single digit finance charges and saving up to $10,000 dollars. Patience pays! Refer to Good Credit or "A" type credit in Chapter Three.

Your last resort should be the Mom and Pop used car lot where your down payment is the price they paid for the car. Trying to get Mom and Pop to put your payment history into your credit file is another story.

Some consumers with a bad credit file have someone with a good credit file finance the car in their name. The consumer with a bad credit file is added to their auto insurance policy. Have a close friend or family with a good credit record buy the vehicle you want to purchase. You pay the monthly payments and your portion of the insurance. You should make a generous down payment. You will save thousands in interest by having somebody with a good credit file put the vehicle in their name.

If you use them as a co-signer you will still have to pay a high finance charges. If you tell a car dealership that you are using someone to finance the vehicle for you, the dealership will throw you out the front door. They call this a *straw purchase*. It is not allowed, even though consumers do it every day. If you go into a bank and tell the loan officer you are using someone to finance the vehicle, the loan officer at the bank might give you the loan. I consulted with several loan officers on this issue. My close friend that owns a dealership said it was illegal. Several other professionals told me it was legal. This technique is based on my research.

My best advice is: if you do this, keep your mouth shut. If you ever had a vehicle repossessed, do not ask anyone to do this for you. Using someone to finance a vehicle for you is used by honest consumers that are gainfully employed and legitimately have a bad credit file.

When using this technique to finance an automobile or any other property, always pay by check or money order and keep your canceled checks and any other evidence. You might need them as evidence to support your credit rating. This is a nontraditional way of building a credit rating that the credit bureaus do not see.

Never finance a vehicle through an automobile promoter. Whenever you go through a third party to finance anything, you usually end up getting ripped-off. Automobile promoters are in the business of acquiring a vehicle from the original owner and then selling or subleasing the car to someone else. The vehicle still remains in the name of the original owner or lessee. The original owner can come over and drive off in the car you think is yours. He can legally drive off in the car, because the creditor did not authorize transfer of ownership. Auto promoting is illegal. In some states, auto promoting is a felony. Creditors and consumers get ripped off in auto promoting.

Save some money and be your own automobile promoter, legally. Use the newspaper classified section or a free paper to find consumers that are behind on their auto payment. This could be an opportunity for you to reestablish credit and purchase a vehicle. When you find and ad in the paper that says, "Take over payments" or "Behind on car note," respond to the ad. When you call the phone number, make sure it is not an automobile promoter. If it is a promoter, hang-up on them. If it is an individual, start asking questions. You can start by asking preference questions, like the color of the car. After you're through with the first round of questions, start on the second round.

What is the interest rate on the loan? You do not want to pay sky-high finance charges. You can get high interest rates anywhere.

How much are your payments and how long? A sensible question. Compare the overall numbers to what the dealership offered you.

How far behind are you on the car note? This is your down payment. This question will tell you how much money you will have to come up with to make the car loan current and how desperate the creditor is. The creditor does not want to repossess the car, especially if the car is worth less than what the outstanding balance on the loan is. Nobody wants to pay more for a car than what it is worth. Bad for the creditor. Bad for the current owner. Two bad marks equal a good for the consumer with a bad credit file. You are more interested in the finance charges and reestablishing credit. Do not feel bad about taking over payments of a car that is worth less than what is owed on it. The majority of the brand-new cars that leave the dealership's are worth less than what is owed on the new car the day it leaves the lot. If you do some math and compare the total cost of the car, including finances charges, you should still save thousands of dollars because of the high interest rate a dealership will stick you with.

Who is the creditor that financed the car? You are going to call the creditor and talk to them about your personal finances, including your credit history. You want the creditor to approve you for the low interest loan. This is another reason to have copies of your credit reports.

Primary and Co-Signer

A co-signer or co-applicant is the consumer that guarantees a debt for the primary applicant. If the primary defaults on the loan, the co-signer is liable to pay the loan as agreed in the contact.

Even with a co-signer, a bad credit file will increase your finance charges. I did not find a single consumer who had actually used it. Several loan officers at different banks told me this: if you want the benefits of loan approval and lower finance charges when financing a car through a bank, the consumer (you) with a bad credit file could apply as the co-applicant instead of the primary applicant. The consumer with a good credit file applies as the primary applicant instead of the co-signer. It is the opposite of having someone cosign for you. You are cosigning for them. The benefits are:

1. Finances charges are not as high, because you are second in command, as the co-signer.
2. Both the primary and co-signer are reported to the credit bureaus by the bank.

3. You have a legal interest in the car. The biggest disadvantage: you are not the owner. This technique
is great with another family member or close
friend, a piggyback ride.

Clean Up Your Credit File
(If you want to re-establish credit after bankruptcy)

Bankruptcy is public records information. For this reason, you
have to get all three copies of your credit reports and clean them
up. Creditors will report your accounts as collection accounts. All
your accounts that were included or completed through bankruptcy should state they were completed or included in bankruptcy. Creditors will think you are still liable for the collection
accounts. Your best evidence in a bankruptcy dispute is to send to
the credit bureaus a copy of the schedule in your petition that lists
all the creditors included in your bankruptcy.

Make sure you get copies of all your credit reports and dispute
any information that is not complete and accurate. Do not pay off
any charge-off or collection accounts until you are sure they are
holding you back from obtaining the type of credit you want. Paying off charge-off or collection accounts will not start your seven
years all over again like in the past. Refer to Chapter Six, Legal
And Illegal Techniques Of Credit Clinics.

If you think charge-offs or collection accounts are costing you
more in finance charges when you obtain credit, you are going to
have to do some math to see if it is worth paying off the charge-
off or collection accounts. Figure your finance charges minus the
finance charges you would have to pay if you paid off the collection account.

You're asking yourself, "How do I know what my finance
charges would be if I paid-off the collection account?" Ask the
creditor where you are applying for credit. Re-establishing credit
might be more beneficial than paying off collection or charge-off
accounts.

When are the collection accounts or charge-offs going to be removed from your credit file? We will see in the next two chapters, Chapters Five and Six.

Another Chapter
On Credit Reports:
Your Credit File

The terms *credit file*, *credit profile* or *credit report* are used interchangeably in this chapter.

Your credit report contains personal data, employment information, your credit history, public records information, and inquiries.

Personal data includes your name, address, previous address, Social Security number, marital status and date of birth.

Employment information includes present and previous employment.

The majority of the information on your credit report is your *credit history*, which includes your account information, payment history to creditors, balances, credit limits and data of this type. Negative information remains in your credit file for seven years. The credit bureaus state that positive information can remain in your credit file indefinitely. Just like negative information, positive information also comes off in seven years. The truth is, the credit bureaus retain *all* the information that they ever received about you. This unlimited time information is only available in very limited circumstances, and it is not worth worrying about.

Public records information is obtained from the public records office. This is information that goes through the courts, including lawsuits, judgments, bankruptcy, liens, child support delinquencies and items of this nature. This type of information remains in your credit file for seven years. Chapter 7, 11, and 12 bankruptcies remain for ten years. A criminal record is public records information as well. The credit bureaus do not report criminal records to creditors. Employers are more interested in a criminal record. Criminal records do not take much effort to obtain.

Inquiries include companies, usually creditors—sometimes employers and insurance companies, who requested a copy of your credit report during the previous two years. Every time you apply for credit, you will add an inquiry to your credit report. Do not add an inquiry to your credit report unless you have to. Creditors frown at desperation. These inquiries can affect your credit rating.

Other inquiries include businesses that are not reported to companies requesting your credit file. The majority of these businesses are credit grantors trying to sell you credit. These are promotional inquiries and do not hurt your credit file. These are some of the businesses that send you all the junk mail.

As you can see, there is more in your credit report than your credit history. If you have seen the statistics of some of the surveys on the accuracy of consumers credit reports, you know that the three major credit bureaus receive several hundred thousand complaints each month because of incorrect and out-of-date information. I believe that every consuming American adult should obtain a copy of their credit reports to verify the accuracy, even if they do not use credit. Your credit report could be merged or have false information on it. It is a slim possibility, but you could be a fraud victim. Your credit report is a part of your personal profile. Your current or prospective employer might want to see your credit report. A good credit report will help you obtain all types of loans. Consumers with bad credit ratings are usually the ones with the most errors in their credit file.

The credit bureaus are not affiliated with our Federal Government. The credit bureaus are regulated by our Federal Government. There are hundreds of credit bureaus. We will concentrate on the three major credit bureaus: *Experian*, formerly known as *TRW, Equifax*, and *Trans Union*. All the hundreds of minor credit bureaus obtain their data from the big three. Credit bureaus are clearing houses of information, in the business of making money on information about you. They sell the information on you to lending institutions, insurance companies, renters, employers and to you. These are some of the same sources they use to obtain data about you. Whenever you fill out a credit application, the information is reported to the credit bureaus. If you close a credit card account, the credit card creditor will inform all nationwide credit bureaus that you closed the account. The credit bureaus will change your credit report to say *account closed by consumer.* Your closed credit card account statement will stay in your credit file seven years from the day you closed the account.

The credit bureaus do not have any authority to approve your loan application. The creditors uses the information supplied by the credit bureaus to make that decision.

Obtaining a copy of your credit report does not take much effort. In the past, the big three credit bureaus changed addresses and had their phone numbers disconnected at their own discretion. This was not fair trade to the consumer who they sell information about. I have included their most recent toll-free numbers. To request a copy by mail, call any of the big three and they will provide you with their current mailing addresses. If you have a Master Card or Visa, you can obtain a copy over the phone or Internet from Experian and Equifax. Because of security reasons, I strongly recommend that you order your credit report by mail and not though the Internet at this time. The maximum your credit report will cost you is $8.00 for each credit report. In a few states, your report will cost less than $8.00. When you call the toll-free number, you will know how much your credit report will cost or if you qualify for a free credit report. I remember when credit reports were two or three times that price. Our government made a law that regulates how much the credit bureaus can charge you for your credit report.

It is my understanding that the big three will retain these toll-free numbers, even if their address changes.

To obtain copies of your credit reports, contact:

Equifax, (800)-685-1111 or www.equifax.com.
Experian (formerly TRW), (800)-682-7654,
www.experian.com.
Trans Union, (800)-916-8800 or www.tuc.com.

You can make your own request form by typing it or simply printing your name, address, social security number, date of birth and proof of residence. You have to stop and think about the information you write on the request form for your credit report. Remember that any of your creditors can obtain this information. For example, if your telephone number is unlisted and you do not want collectors or creditors calling you, write *no phone number available* or *N/A*, even though the credit bureaus ask for your phone number, employer and proof of residence. These three are optional. There are consumers who are unemployed and do not have a phone number. Credit bureaus ask for a copy of your driver's licence or a utility stub to protect you from fraud and to find out where consumers who are hiding out from creditors and collectors live. I do not recommend consumers hide from collectors or creditors, but that is not for me to decide. If you're hiding out from creditors, your credit reports will show this. On your request form simply write, "I do not have a phone number, job or driver license and I live at granny's house." No matter what your personal financial condition is, you and every other consuming American have a right to obtain copies of credit reports. At the same time, the credit bureaus have the responsibility of protecting every consuming American's credit file. If you have nothing to hide from the credit bureaus, then do not hide it.

Your credit report will be processed as soon as the credit bureaus receive your request form along with your personal check or money order. They do not wait for your personal check to clear. By sending a money order (if you have debt collectors trying to collect a debt), you do not have to worry about your checking account information being passed on.

Experian (formerly TRW) stopped providing one free credit report per year to anyone requesting it. You can obtain a free copy of your credit report if you have been denied credit, employment, or insurance in the past 60 days. Under the new *Fair Credit Report Act* that went into law September 30, 1997, you can obtain a free credit report if you are unemployed and plan to apply for a job within the next 60 days, if you receive government assistance or if you think your report contains errors due to fraud.

> *Confidential Credit* offers one-stop shopping for all three credit reports. You will have to contact the credit bureaus independently if you are disputing information from the credit report you purchased from Confidential Credit. Overnight express for all three reports costs $49.95, shipping included. Regular first-class mail for all three reports runs $30.95, shipping included.
> (800) 443-9342.

Under the New Fair Credit Reporting Act, you can dispute inaccurate information at one credit bureau. If the information you disputed is inaccurate, the business supplying the information must notify all nationwide credit bureaus about the inaccurate information and have it corrected. Remember, I said the business supplying the information, not the credit bureaus. The big three credit bureaus do not share information—the creditors supplying the information distribute it to each of the big three credit bureaus. If it is public records information you are disputing, then you will have to take up the dispute with each of the big three credit bureaus. I recommend you to obtain a copy of all three credit reports individually from Experian, Equifax and Trans Union. All three will include instructions on how to read your credit report and a request form in order for you to dispute incorrect and out-of-date information. Each credit bureau has its own name for the form you use to dispute information. I will use the most common terminology and call it a *research request form*. Do not be surprised if you find errors on each credit report from the big three credit bureaus.

After verifying or correcting your credit report from each of the big three, you can obtain a copy from each of the big three at your preference. Some consumers obtain copies semiannually, annually or every three years. I advise consumers to obtain a copy 180 days before applying for a major loan, and sometimes for employment or insurance purposes. Do not join a credit reporting service or fraud protection service. The banks and credit bureaus will offer free promotional services in order to entice the consumer into joining their services. You can take advantage of the free stuff, then cancel the service.

After you obtain a copy of your credit report, you will need to know how to read it. No one knows your credit report better than you do. All you need to know is how to understand it. You do not need to pay someone to do this. Credit reports are not that hard to comprehend. Credit bureaus have made it easier to understand. If you still have trouble comprehending it or disputing information, call the credit bureau that produced your report. They are required by law to help you. Or have a friend or a family member help you.

If your dispute is supported by evidence, send it in along with your research request form. If you send copies of any evidence along with your dispute, you can save a lot of trouble. Think, look and dig for evidence. On your research request form and any additional information you send to the credit bureaus, remember to type or print neatly, make copies for yourself, and send by certified mail 'return receipt requested.' If the credit bureau discovers that the disputed information you returned to them on the research request form is inaccurate, incomplete or cannot be verified, they have to delete the disputed item or modify it to be accurate.

Credit bureaus will check the information you are disputing at no cost to you. They have a 30 calendar day time limit to resolve your dispute.

If they do not settle your dispute in the required time limit, they have to delete it from your credit file. You need to wait a few more days after the 30 calendar day time limit for the mail to run. If you do not receive information about your dispute being investigated, then make a copy of your certified mail receipt and write a letter demanding that the disputed information be removed due to the 30 calendar day time limit.

If you provided additional information during your 30-day time referring to your original dispute, the credit bureaus have 15 more days to settle.

In the past, the credit bureaus had a bad reputation for handling disputed information. This is one of the reasons for the new Fair Credit Reporting Act. Under this law, the credit bureaus will establish a better reputation and follow the laws that govern them.

Credit bureaus cannot reinsert the deleted dispute into your credit file like they used to do to consumers in the past. If the party supplying the information shows proof that the deleted item is complete and accurate and you are notified, the disputed information *can* be reinserted into your credit file. Anytime a dispute changes your credit report, the credit bureau has to furnish you with an updated copy.

If you cannot get your dispute corrected, you can add a hundred word statement to your credit report. For several reasons, the hundred word statement is not that beneficial. Besides, anything could change. You're better off discussing the dispute with your potential creditor yourself or including a statement along with any evidence on your personal loan application. Consumers will put statements in their credit files because of bankruptcy, divorce and fraud victims. If you're still determined on inserting a hundred word statement into your credit file and you need help, the law requires the credit bureaus to assist you. A friend of mine put a statement in his credit file demanding any creditor to call his home phone number before issuing any credit in his name. This is how he protects his credit file.

Several creditors use a scoring system supplied by the credit bureaus. These creditors might not see your hundred word statement or your actual credit file. The most popular scoring system used by the credit bureaus has *ten* different models for the same score or loan. You will be classified in one of the ten models. Each model has a different formula in order to classify you in the right model. The credit bureaus do not throw everybody in the same group. For example, a consumer with an old bankruptcy but no other indication of risk in his credit file might end up with a higher score than a consumer with no negative information in his credit file. FICO credit scores above 660 are considered good scores. The majority of creditors still want to look at the actual credit report.

If the credit bureaus determine your dispute is foolish or irrelevant, they can terminate your investigation. An example of something foolish would be to dispute everything on your credit report—positive and negative information—hoping to overload them with work and to get your credit file cleared because it would be too troublesome to check. An example of something irrelevant would be a dispute where you did not write down all the required information in order to investigate your dispute.

If you're worried about your current or potential employer obtaining a copy of your credit report without your permission, that is 'past history' under the new Fair Credit Reporting Act. Employers must get written authorization from you to obtain your credit or medical report. The new Fair Credit Reporting Act that went into law September 30, 1997 holds credit bureaus more accountable for the information they sell about you and the new law has added *more* protection for your privacy. Under the new law, you can stop the credit bureaus from selling your name and address to inquiries from such creditors as those trying to sell you credit cards. The credit bureause must provide an (800) toll-free number solely for this purpose.

You can contact the credit bureaus to remove your name and address from the big three's lists for unsolicited credit and insurance offers for two years. If you complete and return an "opt-out" form provided on request from the big three, you will be off these lists permanently.

Stop sending me credit card offers and other junk mail.

- Equifax Options, (800)556-4711.

- Trans Union, (800)680-7293.

- Experian Credit Marketing "OPT-OUT", (800) 353-0809.

I was going to enclose a copy of the new Fair Credit Reporting Act but I was persuaded by the consumers' to keep the legal jargon out of this book because very few read it. Anybody can get a copy of the Fair Credit Reporting Act from the Federal Trade Commission by calling them. You will find their number in the back of this publication.

In the next chapter we will go into more detail on disputing information. We will also clarify the legal and illegal techniques used by credit clinics.

By the way, my favorite credit bureau is Experian. After you read Chapter Six, you might find that hard to believe.

Legal And Illegal
Techniques
Of Credit Clinics

In this chapter, we will examine the legal (and illegal) techniques that credit clinics use to charge you hundreds to thousands of dollars to repair your credit.

You can do almost everything yourself that a credit repair clinic can do for you—legally—for just the price of a certified letter. If you feel you need professional help, use an attorney, not a credit repair clinic. Attorneys have a lot more to lose than a credit repair clinic. Do not risk losing your money by using a credit repair clinic. Through your local bar association, you can find an attorney that specializes in credit restoration. There are bankruptcy attorneys that do credit repair as well. There are reputable credit consultants that have been successful at removing or correcting negative items from a consumer's credit file, but they're few and far between. If you hire someone to remove negative information from your credit file, never give the professional more than a very small retainer fee. After the negative items are permanently removed or corrected in your credit file, pay the balance. There are no guarantees that you or anybody else can remove a negative item from your credit file.

Several factors will determine if your negative item will be removed or not. These factors include accuracy, timing, employees, creditors, account balances and other factors. Reading the rest of this chapter should help you decide what to do.

You will see advertisements saying, "We remove bankruptcy, judgments, charge-offs, collection accounts, liens..." This is not false advertising. In the majority of cases, they remove this information because it is almost time to be removed, it is past time to be removed, or the consumer pays off the debt. Then the negative item is removed from the consumer's credit file. Bankruptcy, judgements and liens are public records information. Anybody and their Grandma can go down to the public records office or County Court House and hand the clerk a piece of paper with your name and address on it to see if you have a judgment against you. I have seen public records information removed from a consumer's credit file before it was time to be removed. As I explained earlier, it was almost time for the information to be removed. It is a hassle for credit bureaus to verify public records information. Public records information might not be in your credit file at one of the credit bureaus, but it is still available to other sources, including the public. If the information is not in your credit file, then no creditor will see it.

Delinquencies are payments made 30 to 180 days after the due dates. Delinquencies are the same as being late—they just sound worse. If delinquencies are complete and accurate, they will remain in your credit file for seven years from the date of the late payment. This is true even if you later bring your payments current.

Collection accounts are accounts that have not had any activity for three to six months or longer. If collection accounts are complete and accurate, they will remain in your credit file seven years from the date of the original late payment. *Charge-offs* are when the creditor writes off the account, instead of turning it over to collections. You are still liable for charge-offs just like collection accounts. If charge-offs are complete and accurate, they will remain in your credit file for seven years from the date of the original late payment.

Starting January 1998, all creditors will be required to report the date of the first late payment. This starts your seven-year time period ticking.

Charge-offs, collection accounts and bankruptcies are considered *derogatory items.*

Collection accounts and charge-offs are the result of an unsecured debt that were not paid as agreed. It is important for you to know that the new Fair Credit Reporting Act states that once the delinquent account becomes a collection account or charge-off, the seven-year period started ticking the day the first payment was late and does not stop ticking for seven years when the item can come off the credit report.

In the past, if the consumer paid any amount toward the collection account or charge-off, the seven-year period would start all over again. Now you can pay off your collection account or charge-off and your seven-year reporting period started the day the account was originally late. Once your account goes past delinquent and into collection or charge-off, your seven-year reporting period in your credit file started the day your payment was late. This is good for the consumer and creditor. If you continue to pay your account when it is delinquent, your seven-year period continues to roll. In other words you are basically still paying as agreed, but not on time. Once your account goes past delinquent, it does not go back to delinquent. Do not sign a new agreement with the creditor or collector after your account goes past delinquent unless you know exactly what you are signing.

Statutes Of Limitation

Something else might mean more to you than the seven-year mark in your credit report and the majority of consumers do not realize it when dealing with collection accounts and charge-offs. Creditors and collectors hate it: the *statute of limitations* in your state for an *open-ended account* or *open account*.

An example of an open account is a credit card loan. The statute of limitations is the maximum number of years a creditor has to sue you if your debt goes unpaid. Consumers pay off collection accounts and charge-offs every day which they do not need to because the statute of limitations expired for the open account.

Consumers pay off these accounts because the accounts still appear on their credit reports.

Consumers also pay off these accounts when they are not on their credit reports. Even though an account was removed from their credit file, a collector kept an eye on their credit report for any activity (actually the computer was keeping an eye on any credit activity). When the collector spotted the activity, he called the consumer for payment. All the consumer had to say to the collector was, "I have an absolute defense—the statute of limitations expired."

The time-limit on the statute of limitations varies from state to state. In 49 states (including the District of Colombia), the statute of limitations is 3 to 6 years for open accounts. The statutes of limitations on written contracts and promissory notes will expire with the same time limitations as open accounts or later, depending on what state you live in.

The statute of limitations does not cause your debt to blow away in the wind after it expires. If the creditor files suit, the consumer has an absolute defense. The consumer must offer the new evidence to avoid a judgement. The evidence will consist of papers the consumer files to support his claim. If the creditor sues you, and you do not prove to the court that the statute of limitations expired, you will have a lost lawsuit and a judgement against you.

Why wait for the creditor to sue you? Get the name and address of the collection agency or creditor that owns your collection account. Your credit report from Experian will provide you with the name and address or you can use the sample letter at the end of this chapter to get the name and address of the creditor or collector. Send a certified letter (return receipt requested) to the collection agency or creditor stating that the statute of limitations has expired for your open account. Ask for a response. This does not mean they cannot sue you, but it will be evidence that you might want to show somebody one day.

Remember, you can sue anybody for anything. If you start rebuilding your credit, you will have activity in your credit file and the collector will be aware that you know the statute of limitations expired for the debt or open account. The certified letter might come in handy one day for other reasons. The odds of you being sued for an open account after the statute of limitations expired is slim, but possible. Just knowing the statute of limitations expired can get a monkey off your back.

Depending on what state you live in, if you make a partial payment, you could be extending your statute of limitations on your collection account or charge-off. A collector might call you one day and say you waived your rights when you made a deal with the collection agency. Do not take anything for granted a collector tells you. Make them prove it to you, in or out of court. For about half the population, the statute of limitations started ticking the day you made the last payment for the account. Use the back of the book and call your attorney general's office or an attorney in your state to learn about your statute of limitations for open accounts.

Besides finding out about the expiration in the statute of limitations in your state, you need to know if your state requires a written promise to pay in order to *extend* the statute of limitations. Some mortgage companies will overlook a collection account or charge-off if the statute of limitations expired. Why? The creditor will not be able to put a lien against the home if you assert your right because the statute of limitations expired. You might have to bring this up to the mortgage company.

You might be asking yourself, "It has been such a long time since my "open account" has had any activity that I do not know when my statute of limitations started ticking." Use your credit report as a reference. Your credit report will tell you the date of last activity for your account. You will have your credit report with the date of last activity and a certified letter stating that the statute of limitations expired.

From my studies, I found that if a debtor files bankruptcy and the creditor lets the statute of limitations expire, the creditor loses the right to make a claim in bankruptcy court. Makes sense, doesn't it? If the creditor does not have an enforceable claim in state court because the statute of limitations expired, then why should the creditor have an enforceable claim in bankruptcy court?

Even though a debt is an absolute promise to pay, if the statute of limitations expired and the creditor tries to make you live up to the debt, you have the right not to fulfill the promise (debt). How you handle your accounts is totally up to you to decide. At the same time, it is only fair that you know your legal rights. Enough on the statute of limitations. Time to move on.

NOTE: If you have a collection account or charge-off in your credit file that is over seven years old, make the information provider remove it by disputing it with the research request form provided by the credit bureau.

In some cases, you will have a *deficiency balance*. This is the result of a collateralized loan that was repossessed or foreclosed. As with a repossessed car or foreclosed home, you still owe a debt to the creditor for the difference from what the collateral was sold for and what you owed the creditor.

Disputing Information

Credit bureaus are not working for you and me. They are working for the creditors. It is possible to have a negative item removed from your credit file and still owe the debt. *No federal law requires negative information to remain in your credit file for seven to ten years.* The federal law states the *maximum* negative information can remain in your credit file is seven to ten years. If it were up to the creditors and credit bureaus, the negative information would stay in your credit file until the day you went to heaven. You have the right to dispute incomplete and inaccurate information. You are not breaking the law when you dispute information in your credit file. If anybody tells you that you're breaking the law, they are being financed by the credit bureaus or creditors. You can also waste a lot of your time and effort disputing information that you know should be in your credit file.

The key word is *accurate*. You do not have to lie when disputing a negative item. Credit reports are full of errors. If you look close enough you might find something that is technically inaccurate with the negative item. You have a right to dispute a negative item that is partially right as long as you believe the negative item is not complete and accurate. This technique can also be used by a consumer who feels the negative information in the credit file is questionable. "Questionable" usually means a small *collection account* that is several years old and cannot be identified by the consumer. There are thousands of consumers with small questionable collection accounts.

Some businesses do not keep information as long as the credit bureaus do. Some businesses might find it to be too much trouble to investigate the dispute. Remember, if the credit bureaus cannot verify the disputed information to be complete and accurate, they must remove the disputed information. The credit bureaus must meet the 30-day time limit. It is easier to have inaccurate information removed by a smaller creditor because smaller creditors do not retain information as efficiently or as long as a large creditor. Large commercial creditors like big banks retain negative information as long and as efficiently as the credit bureaus do, even though they are not required to.

Remember, credit bureaus keep negative or positive information for seven years except for Chapter 7, 11 and 12 bankruptcies which they keep for 10 years.

It costs money to investigate a negative item. When disputing a small collection account or a late payment that is a few years old, the odds are in your favor. You are wasting your time disputing everything at the same time.

- Dispute one negative item at a time and space your disputes out. This is why it can take over a year to correct several negative items from one credit report.

- Keep good records of how long it has been since you initiated the dispute. Do not forget that the 30-day time limit is a factor.

- Do not use the research request form you received from the credit bureau when disputing items of this nature. Use the sample letter at the end of this Chapter.

As we learned earlier, under the new Fair Credit Reporting Act you can dispute inaccurate information at one credit bureau. If the information you disputed is modified, the business supplying the information must notify all credit bureaus about the corrected information. If the negative item is not removed from your credit file, try something different, like moving on to the information provider. You can write to the business that is supplying the credit bureaus with the negative information.

The business supplying the negative information is the information provider. The information provider is the creditor or collection agency. You can write to the information provider and ask to see the evidence that supports their claim. Make the information provider show you the evidence that supports the negative information you are disputing. The law requires the information to be *complete and accurate*. Due to several factors, the creditor or collection agency might not be able to supply complete and accurate evidence to support their claim. With all the advanced software and computer technology, human error and laziness still play a role in the negative information being removed.

If the information provider makes *any* change that affects your dispute, they must inform all nationwide credit bureaus. If the negative information is not removed because the information provider supplied you with complete and accurate information, you can go to the next level and negotiate the account.

Collection accounts in this publication refer to charge-offs as well, unless I note specifically otherwise. *You do not need a credit repair clinic to negotiate your collection account.* Credit repair clinics and collectors will feel you out to see how much money you have, and how much it means for you to have the collection account paid off. Do not tell a collector or anyone else trying to collect a debt from you your personal business. If you tell them you are paying off the collection account to purchase a specific home, that is a giveaway that you are good for the total collection account. Tell them the only reason that you're thinking about paying it off is that you know of collection accounts that were settled for a fraction of the totaled owed—if you can settle your collection account for a small percentage of the totaled owed, then you will settle the collection account. Otherwise, forget about it.

Collection agencies only have a 25% chance of collecting an account that is over a year old. Theoretically that means if you owe one thousand dollars for the collection account and it is a year old, it is only worth two hundred and fifty dollars today. Keep your negotiations with the collection agency or creditor simple; make them an offer in writing. Tell the collector to take it or leave it, and to please leave you alone. Keep it short and sweet. Being patient is not only a virtue, it is your best negotiating tool. Rarely do debtors or collectors experience patience. That is why you should start negotiating your account as far in advance as possible. You can always raise your offer, but do not raise your offer too soon. Wait for the collection agency to call you.

If your collection account is still in the hands of the original credit card creditor, or their in-house collection department, you might have a harder time trying to negotiate the collection account. Some of these big banks will not take any less than the amount owed, but will sell your collection account for a discount to an outside collection agency. The big banks will sell your collection account to someone else for a discount, but not to you! Remember that when dealing with debt that can be discharged, it is *negotiable debt*. I gave you a starting point on negotiating.

Settling a collection account or charge-off occurs when you pay it off. You are no longer liable for the debt. I would never sign anything a collector asks me to sign—I would just agree to pay the charge-off or collection account.

Even though large credit card creditors will work with you when negotiating payment arrangements, large credit card creditors and their in-house collection departments are the hardest to deal with when it comes to settling collection accounts and removing the negative items from your credit report. The way you deal with large credit card creditors after you settle the collection account is a little different. If the creditor did not agree to remove the negative item from your credit file after you settle the collection account, then you can start disputing the negative item directly with the credit bureaus. If you're persistent in your disputes to the credit bureaus, the creditor has no reason to keep the negative item in your credit file, because the account has been settled.

Do not take anybody for their word. You need to do all your negotiations through the mail. If they make any promises, you will have evidence in writing to hold the creditor or collector to their word. Do not make any oral contracts. For example, if the creditor or collector agrees to completely remove the negative item (collection account) from your credit file after you pay it off, get it in writing. You will have a signed and written agreement as evidence to support your claim. If the creditor lollygags around or does not hold up to their word, you can send copies of your letter to the credit bureaus.

I was informed by a friend that some creditors have a commitment with the credit bureaus that a negative item will not be removed until it is time for the negative item to be removed. I asked her, "What if the negative item is not complete and accurate?" Do not let that stop you from disputing negative information that is not complete and accurate.

Do not spend any more money on repairing your credit file than you have to. You have to ask yourself, "Why are you paying off the collection account or accounts?" Do you need the negative items like a collection account or charge-off removed from your credit file? If you have collection accounts, charge-offs and delinquencies in your credit file, then you should *visit the moon*. Visiting the moon means having the collection accounts and charge-offs removed from your credit file.

If you have recent positive information in your credit file along with one or two small collection accounts, then having the collection account show "paid collection" or "paid charge-off" will be satisfactory to some creditors, like a mortgage company. In this case, you should shoot for the moon, and if you fall short you can still land on a star. Landing on a star would be to pay off the collection account and *still* have the negative item appear in your credit file. If your goal is to obtain unsecured debt like several unsecured credit cards, all negative information will have to be removed from your credit file—including delinquencies. In other words, you are going to have to be the man on the moon. Being the man on the moon is possible, even though I do not care about going there. Do not spend any more money than you have to when repairing your credit file.

If you settle your collection account for less money than what is actually owed, you could end up owing the IRS a tax liability. If the difference from what you actually owed minus what you paid off the collection account for is over $600, you should get a 1099 from the creditor or collection agency stating how much you have to add as income to your tax return. Making a deal with your creditors or collectors can cost you more money than expected. A consumer asked me if he filed bankruptcy would he owe the IRS for discharging his debts? The answer is no, because it is discharged through bankruptcy.

If you filed for bankruptcy or have other unfavorable credit information you want erased, you might receive a sales pitch from a credit repair clinic saying that you will not be able to obtain a loan for ten years. Information from the credit repair clinic could be misleading (and incorrect).

In some cases, a credit repair clinic will charge you a large fee to tell you to file bankruptcy. Do not let anyone talk you into filing bankruptcy. Do not let anyone talk you out of filing bankruptcy. All the credit repair clinic wants is your money. Credit repair clinics will guarantee you that they will break the law in order to change your credit identity. Why would you trust somebody with your money that guarantees you that they will break the law? When you hire someone to break the law for you, you are breaking the law, too.

File segregation occurs when you establish a new credit identity by using a false Social Security number or employer identification number. Employer Identification numbers are assigned by the Internal Revenue Service for businesses. It is a federal crime to misrepresent your Social Security number on a loan or credit application. Credit clinics will talk consumers into using juveniles, foreigners and their own children's Social Security numbers. Parents can damage their own children's credit file before they become adults.

I can understand a single mother using one of her several children's Social Security number to have the utilities turned on if the single mothers' credit file was damaged due to divorce or other circumstances and she cannot afford the large deposit that is required by some utility companies. When a customer's credit report is bad, some utility companies require a large deposit before the service is turned on. The single mother must provide for herself and the children.

File segregation is promoted by credit clinics, classified ads and all over the Internet. I know some individuals who had bankruptcy in their credit file and used file segregation for a new credit identity. These individuals ended up in the same situation they were in the first time. It did not take them as long, and it was worse the second time. Not only did they cheat creditors out of money, they started conning money out of anyone that was gullible. These file segregation individuals would have been better off to re-establish credit after bankruptcy. When you break the law the first time, it is always easier to break the law a second time, and it just gets worse from there. People use file segregation to hide their identity as well as their property from creditors and collectors. File segregation might bring short-term capital but can bring long-term consequences that are not in your favor. I am not speaking for everyone in writing about file segregation. I am speaking only from my experiences.

Some companies in business for over ten years will sell file segregation for one hundred and fifty dollars. The loopholes the companies work through are beyond the scope of this publication. The credit repair clinic is sending you the information to break a federal law. Even if you filed your new Employer Identification number under a "Sub-Chapter S Corp," at some point the credit bureaus will red-flag your credit file.

If you have filed bankruptcy recently, you might be a target for the segregation promotion. I promise you that it is a lot easier to re-establish credit after bankruptcy than credit clinics tell you (and what the public realizes). An individual would want to use file segregation only because he intends to break the law, not only by using file segregation but also for other illegal activities associated with it.

If you finance a home, you do not want to put a Social Security number that is not yours on the mortgage account.

Everybody has a right for a second chance. Do it legally.

Sample Letter (Information in parentheses is for your use only.)

Name of Credit Bureau
Address of Credit Bureau
City, State and Zip.
ATT: Consumer Assistance Department

      Your Name
      S.S.#
      Address
      City, State and Zip.
      Date of Birth

Consumer Assistance Department:
      I do not agree with the negative information in my credit report that (name of credit bureau) is supplying to businesses. This incorrect item is extremely damaging to my credit rating. I want the account listed below to be investigated immediately.
      (In this space write down what is wrong with the negative information—for example, one or more of the following:

      1. You are not being supplied with accurate information from the information provider.

      2. This account is not mine.

      3. I have paid as agreed and on time.

      4. These are not my inquiries and I want them removed.)

      Please provide me with the employee's name and address of the information provider you used to verify the above information. (Experian includes the addresses of the information providers on their credit reports. Ask for the address anyway along with the name of the employees for the information provider and credit bureau that are handling your dispute.) Please provide me with the name of the individual handling my dispute at _____(name of credit bureau).
      Thank you for your immediate assistance.

Sincerely,

      Your Name (Signature)
      (End of Letter)

If you are not pleased with the credit bureau's service, you should complain to the attorney general's office in your state. The Federal Trade Commission is swamped with complaints from consumers. You might not hear from the Federal Trade Commission until a new law is enacted.

You can complain to the Federal Trade Commission by making a simple phone call. It is well worth doing if you have a legitimate beef. The FTC's phone numbers are in back of the book.

If you want to help change the law, send a complaint to the Federal Trade Commission as well. This is how new federal laws that favor consumers develop.

Debt Consolidation Programs Are They For You?

Debt management programs offer services to *consolidate* your debt. I refer to them as nice collection agencies that work for the big banks.

If you're overburdened with credit card debt and thinking about joining a company offering to consolidate your debt with a 20%-50% cut in your monthly credit card payments, you need to read this entire publication.

Take for example somebody who has a considerable amount of unsecured debt—several credit cards close to or at their limits. They have a car note, a mortgage or rent payment. All their obligations are paid on time, but they feel like they are somewhat strapped at the end of the month. In other words, their debt-to-income ratio is on the high side but not out of control.

These people could (possibly) obtain a consolidation loan from a lending institution, family member or friend. If they were able to borrow the money without collateral from a lending institution such as a bank or credit union, the interest rate would probably be as high as the credit card interest rate or higher. Even if they did obtain the consolidation loan—no matter the source or interest rate—the situation could worsen in the future by using credit cards to acquire more debt on top of the consolidation loan.

Collateralizing the loan could jeopardize the collateral. If you know you will not use your credit cards to acquire more debt (and can obtain the consolidation loan at a lower interest rate, or a no-interest loan from a friend or family member), the option I am about to explain to you is worth considering.

Of all the people I know who obtained a consolidation loan, only a few of them did not accumulate more debt with the use of their credit cards. I have concluded that, no matter the situation, *you should not try to borrow your way out of debt.*

You got yourself in this situation. You should get yourself out. Debt management programs offer to consolidate your debt. They can help people in a credit card debting situation and can save some money. Being in a debt management program can educate you on personal finances and help you retain a good credit report.

This is how it works. You get in contact with one of the *credit counselors* at the debt management organization. They will discuss your situation and mail you the required paper work. You fill it out and send to your creditors, and back to the debt management organization. You make one payment every month to the debt management organization. You are a client. They will divide your single payment up accordingly and distribute it to your creditors.

The majority of the creditors will not let you use your credit cards that are included in the program. In return, you may benefit from reduced or waived finance charges. With reduced or waived finance charges and lower minimum monthly payment granted by some creditors, you could find your self saving money on a monthly basis at the same time paying off more toward your principal.

Some individuals will retain one of their credit cards or obtain a debit card depending on the their needs.

You will usually remain in the debt management program from 3 to 5 years. After you become a client of a debt management program, you need to get in contact with each lending institutions that issued you credit and make sure you are receiving the maximum benefits. When I say maximum benefits, I mean finance charges reduced or waived. For example, I have seen where the same bank might waive finance charges to one consumer while the other consumer with the same bank and credit card will not have her finance charges waived. In some cases, all it took to have the individuals finance charges lowered was a phone call to the debt management organization. In other cases, you have to get in contact with the creditor to receive the lowest interest rate possible.

American Express, Discover, Bank of New York, First USA, Bloomingdales and several other retailers will waive finance charges. Sears and several other creditors will not waive finance charges. I believe every creditor should waive finance charges for all consumers in a debt management program. This is debt that can be erased in bankruptcy. In the majority of cases, the creditors have made enough profit off the consumers because of high finance charges.

Before committing to a debt management program, try to find out which one of your creditors will waive finance charges. If you have an available balance on the one that will waive finance charges, transfer the balance of the creditor who will not lower or waive your finance charges.

Creditors will sometimes put a statement in your credit file stating credit counseling next to your account number. Most creditors will disregard this credit counseling statement. What the creditors will look at is your credit history, not a statement. Few creditors will treat the statement saying credit counseling as if you had a recent bankruptcy filing.

Some consumers with a good credit file who are in a debt management program complain to me about having to make a large deposit for new mobile phone service because the credit counseling statement appeared on their credit report. The deposits were as large as a recent bankruptcy consumer would have to make. Mobile phone companies have the most unpaid accounts in the credit industry. All you lose is your mobile phone service if you do not pay—your lights at home stay on. After consulting with the credit department on their true credit history, the mobile phone companies waived the large deposits. The mobile phone companies were basing their credit history on the credit counseling statement, not on their true credit rating. The majority of consumers in debt consolidation programs have tarnished credit reports. A lot of these consumers do not realize that their credit report is tarnished. The banks which issued your credit cards to you want any prospective creditors to see the statement saying "credit counseling" next to your account number in your credit report.

There are hundreds of companies offering debt management services, most are nonprofit organizations. The smaller debt management organizations trying to sell you the hardest also offer the most guarantees and have large up-front fees, so these are the ones you want to stay away from. Some of the smaller ones which will end up costing you more money go through the bigger, more reputable organizations.

Consumer Credit Counseling Services is nationwide and one of the most reputable debt management organizations. You can find a local office in your phone book or call 1-800-388-2227. CCCS counselors will meet you face to face.

Genus Credit Management, formerly NCCS, is another reputable debt management organization. Genus will do everything through the mail out of their central office based in Maryland. Genus' phone number is 1-888-844-6227.

In some cases, when a debt management organization offers to cut your monthly payments 30% to 50%, it can be just as bad to your credit history as a bankruptcy. When your credit card payment is cut in half, your credit card loan turns into an installment loan like an automobile loan. Instead of your credit card payment decreasing each month, because you are not using the credit cards, it stays the same for several years. In your original credit card contract, you are required to pay a percentage of your balance each month. That percentage is usually 48 divided by your balance. As time goes by, your minimum monthly payment will decrease. In a debt consolidation program, your monthly payment stays the same.

Debt management organizations like CCCS would like you to consolidate your debt and be a part of their organization. They usually receive approximately 15 percent of your monthly payment from the creditor, even though they are nonprofit corporations. That does not mean the credit counselors are working for free. This is where the majority of the credit counselors' salaries come from: a portion of your monthly payment. Some employees of these debt management organizations receive incentives. The lending institutions supporting the debt management programs do this in order to benefit their lending institutions. They know if your debting situation deteriorates, they could end up in a worse situation by the consumer filing bankruptcy and the lending institution receiving either pennies on the dollar or nothing at all.

Debt management organizations are basically nice collection agencies working for the creditor. I know consumers who were in a debt management program and still found themselves strapped for money at the end of each month, so they went on to the next level and filed Chapter 7 bankruptcy (liquidation) or Chapter 13 bankruptcy (wage earners plan) to free up a considerable amount of their income. The consumer underestimated expenditures even though they had a credit counselor to help them. The credit counselor did not inform them of other options available.

Other Options: Bankruptcy

One of these options is a Chapter 13 bankruptcy (wage earners plan). I know one consumer who was pinching pennies in order to make her payment to a debt consolidation program. She felt obligated to pay back her creditors what she owed them. I talked her into a Chapter 13 bankruptcy (wage earners plan) and *her monthly expenses dropped over seven hundred dollars a month!* She still has the option of paying back her creditors a hundred percent of the principal in her Chapter 13 plan.

If I were her, I would not pay back any more saturated fat debt in my original Chapter 13 payment plan than what I had to. If you are one of the hundreds of thousands of consumers in a debt management program living below your budget due to credit card

85

debt, and you're struggling to meet your monthly obligations, you should consider a Chapter 13 payment plan.

Chapter 13 Payment Plan

Every one of the consumers in a debt consolidation program- who consulted with me expresses surprise at the difference in their monthly payment. Debt management organizations are nice collection agencies working for the banks. I believe there are hundreds of thousands of consumers who are in a debt management program that should be in a Chapter 13 payment plan.

If you are in a debt management program and it is working out, fine, then stick with it. Whatever you do, take a peek at your credit reports.

What if you're overburdened with debt but you do not want to file any type of bankruptcy? Why let a nonprofit credit counselor paid by the big banks do your budget for you? I would not expose my personal finances to a credit counselor who is financed by the big banks until I knew exactly what I was going to do. You should be using the laws that govern our great country to your favor. Do your own budget or pay an experienced Chapter 13 bankruptcy attorney to help you with it. No one knows a debtor budget better. I wrote an experienced Chapter 13 bankruptcy attorney, not a Chapter 7 bankruptcy liquidator attorney.

Some Chapter 7 bankruptcy attorneys have Chapter 13 experience as well. Read Chapter Eight. It might save you from filing bankruptcy and provide you with more money to make a living on than a debt management program will do for you. You might need to reduce your credit card payments 70% to 90%.

I have been informed that some credit counselors working for these debt management organizations scare consumers about their wages being garnished. In Chapter Eight I will show you how to protect your wages without filing bankruptcy or joining a debt consolidation program.

Depending on your debt load, income, credit rating and what state you live in, a Chapter 13 bankruptcy could be more beneficial to you than being in a debt management program. The major disadvantage of filing a Chapter 13 bankruptcy compared to joining a debt management organization: you will have a Chapter 13 bankruptcy appear on your credit report. Chapter 13 bankruptcy is less damaging to your credit report than Chapter 7 bankruptcy.

Credit bureaus report successfully completed Chapter 13 bankruptcy for *seven years* from the day it was filed. Chapter 7,11 and 12 bankruptcies are reported for *ten years*.

If you are overburdened with debt, delinquent in your accounts, or have collection accounts or charge-off that will appear on your credit report for several years, any one of these three reasons may hold you back from obtaining credit and you might be better off filing a Chapter 13 or Chapter 7. The two most important factors before considering to file for a Chapter 13 bankruptcy are your non-exempt property and excess income, meaning your monthly income minus your monthly expenses.

In a Chapter 13 bankruptcy, you could walk away with all your property and pay back your unsecured creditors a smaller percentage of what you owe them, depending on your excess income and the value of your non-exempt property. A debt management program requires you to pay your creditors in full. In the majority of cases, your debt management payment will include finance charges along with the principal. Chapter 7 and 13 bankruptcies carry more clout and protect you from creditors and collectors from taking action against you. When you are a client of a debt management organization, you do not have this kind of protection from creditors or collectors. Remember, everybody's situation is different and non-exempt property varies greatly from state to state. I will go into more detail on (Chapter 7 and 13) bankruptcies toward the end of this publication.

I recommend debt consolidation programs for consumers with a good credit file who are not overburdened with debt. Some of the consumers I know who are in a debt consolidation program can afford to pay off their credit card loans. They are in the program to taking advantage of the waived or reduced interest rates.

If you decide a debt management program is for you or if you want to take advantage of waived or reduced finance charges, and you have a good credit file that you do not want to tarnished, make sure your payments to the debt management organization is distributed to your creditors before the due date on your credit cards.

Do not go under your minimum monthly payment for each bank that issued you a credit card. For example, if you have two credit card issuing banks included in your monthly payment, the total payment should equal the minimum payment from each of the two banks. The reason for this is the bank will more than likely report you as being late if you do not make your minimum monthly payment. As time passes, your account becomes more and more delinquent. This is one way consumers who joined a debt management program tarnished their credit report. From the date you started in a debt management program to the date you finished a debt management program, the only difference in your credit file should be paid-off credit cards that were in the program. The statement, saying "credit counseling" will be removed from your credit file when you get out of the program. You need to look at your credit reports to make sure that statement is removed.

Credit counseling is not as damaging to your credit file as several accounts showing 60, 90, or 120+ days delinquent. If you cannot afford your minimum monthly payment required by your credit card contract, you might be better off filing a Chapter 13 bankruptcy or a Chapter 7, instead of joining a debt management organization.

What state you live in will make a difference in your decision between bankruptcy and a debt consolidation program. In extreme cases, Consumer Credit Counseling Services will inform a consumer of bankruptcy. Consumer Credit Counseling Services runs ads advertising that bankruptcy is a ten year mistake. Joining a debt management program like CCCS can be a mistake. Consumer Credit Counseling Services would not even exist if it were not for consumer credit card debt. *100% of consumer credit card debt can be discharged in bankruptcy.* Every consumer who discharges credit card debt in bankruptcy is a lost customer for a debt management organization.

Do not let Consumer Credit Counseling Services or any other debt management organization advertisements interfere with your decision on bankruptcy. If it were not for credit card debt, a lot of bankruptcy attorneys would be out of business, too.

Do not let an attorney talk you into bankruptcy. Both debt management organizations and attorneys play a role in helping you take care of yourself financially, but more importantly, *you have to learn how to take care of yourself financially.*

Ask yourself a few questions:

- Am I that far behind on my credit card payments?
- How large of a credit card debt load do I have?
- Is my credit report damaged?
- Will I be able to obtain a mortgage sooner by filing a Chapter 7 bankruptcy?
- Do I care what my credit report looks like?
- Will I be disciplined enough to live on a cash basis?
- What are my alternatives?

My personal opinion follows: debt management programs are for consumers who want out of credit card debt. Because of the freewheeling credit card lending practices, bankruptcy has become the outlet for consumers who need out of credit card debt. Our Congress should establish laws governing credit card debt exclusively. Americans should not risk losing their home or other personal property because of credit card debt unless they used the credit card to purchase the home.

Get Tough With Plastic: Reorganize Your Debt Without Filing Bankruptcy

Now let's learn a little bit about the credit card lending industry and then we will know why we need to get tough with plastic. Statistics in this chapter originate from the United States Government (sorry for sounding so serious—I just wanted you and the "Fat Cats" to know where I got some of my stats). With all that background, we will figure out how to reorganize debt without filing bankruptcy!

Do you know the difference between charge cards and *credit cards?* The first plastic card was known as a *charge card.* Diners Club introduced the first popular charge card in 1950. Charge cards require the owner to pay off the card balance in full when the bill arrives. Charge cards like Diners Club or American Express can be just like credit cards for traveling and entertainment expenses, because you can pay back a little each month for traveling and entertainment expenses.

Paying back a little each month will cause you to carry a balance for traveling and entertainment expenses (while being charged a high interest rate as with a credit card). Charge cards can be credit cards.

MasterCard and Visa represent the two best-known *credit cards.* Credit cards can be used to extend credit in the form of a personal unsecured loan, with regular monthly payments for the loan (or balance). Bank of America issued the first credit card in 1966. This card, now known as Visa, is issued by companies around the world. Banks, department stores and large conglomerates now operate in the credit card business.

Credit card lending *is* big business. The fifty largest credit card lenders hold approximately 80 percent of all credit card loans or what we refer to as credit card balances. In 1995, credit card companies mailed out 2.7 *billion* direct mail solicitations to the American consumer. With their mail solicitation applications, most creditors offered low teaser interest rates between 4.9 and 8.9 percent.

We are all separate individuals and each creditor likewise is a separate company. Although all major creditors follow the same *laws,* not all creditors follow the same *rules.*

Timing & Tools

Timing is an important factor when calling the creditor. Not just anyone who answers the phone can reduce your finance charges. Very few employees have the authority to lower your finance charges unless there is a promotional rate going on at the bank. *The credit card lender does not have to lower your finance charges.* We will do our best to have them waived or reduced.

In Budget Option, you will find that finance charges will not be significant. Since Budget Option is for people with bad credit, your credit report will not be important either. We will cover these items in this chapter where you will learn:

- how to negotiate a lower interest rate and continue to use your current credit card;

- how to give your current credit card back to the creditor and try to have your finance charges reduced or waived—without tarnishing your credit;

- how to stop working for your credit card lenders and stop living for your credit report without filing bankruptcy (because of the bankruptcy laws, this technique carries more clout than any other technique introduced in this chapter).

If you want to keep your credit cards, then you should be the one to negotiate a lower interest rate for your accounts.

If you plan on giving your credit card back to the creditor, you can have someone else negotiate your account for you. In either case, you must let the creditor know who is authorized to represent you. Your representative can be a friend, family member or professional. You can have that same person negotiate your account after it is passed on to a third party.

Most creditors have a *fixed rate* for all accounts passed on to a debt management organization. Only a few creditors will waive finance charges for consumers in a debt management program. In my opinion, all creditors should waive finance charges for consumers who have been good-paying customers for a long time and who *want* to give their credit card back to the consumer. Alas, my opinion does not mean anything to the big banks.

Now for real negotiating tools.

- Your most important negotiating tool is *kindness*.

When you're nice to creditors and collectors, you are also being nice to yourself. Being nice does not mean you have to tell the creditor or collector anything about your personal situation.

- If credit card creditors calls you at work, tell them you will be doing all your negotiating on your home phone or through the mail. They will note your account. Do not wait around to start your negotiations.

Some creditors' in-house collection departments are referred to as the *hardship department*. I usually refer to them as creditors or credit card creditors. A creditor—depending on the status of your account—may refer you to a different department.

- Bankruptcy is a negotiating tool when dealing with credit card debt. If it were not for the bankruptcy laws, credit card debt would not be negotiable debt.
- Credit card debt can be bad debt, no matter what your finance charges. Look over these two Citibank statements. Citibank has issued more credit cards than *any* other creditor. These statements contain the majority of subjects we will cover.

Note that the two statements are a year apart. The 6.9% interest rate was *not* a promotional interest rate. It took several phone calls and several phone negotiations to get down to the 6.9 % interest rate. On some phone calls, the finance charges did not budge; on other phone calls, the finance charges came down some, a little at a time. Each phone call was spread apart a couple of months. It was well worth it because the savings in finance charges were in the thousands.

Look at the balances from one year to the next. You will see that this credit card remained in use while the customer

Table 1: Statement /

09/08/94

	9/06
8/12	8/12
8/12	8/12
8/12	8/12
8/13	8/13
8/13	8/13
8/13	8/13
8/13	8/13
8/13	8/13
8/14	8/14
8/14	8/14
8/14	8/14
8/15	8/15

	Previous Balance	(+) Purchases & Advances	(–) Payments	(–) Credits	(+)FINANCE CHARGE	(+) Late Charges	(=) New Balance		
								Purchases Minimum Due	305.24
								Advances Minimum Due	208.76
Purchases	22503.69	390.82	389.14		131.18		22636.55	Amount Over Credit Line / Fees	
Advances	2141.97		135.86		34.70		2040.81	Past Due	
Total	24645.66	390.82	525.00		165.88		24677.36	Minimum Amount Due	514.00

Rate Summary Number of days this Billing Period 30	Purchases	Advances
Balance Subject to Finance Charge	22814.30	2132.91
Periodic Rate (Purchases-Monthly, Advances-Daily)	.57500%	.05424%
Nominal Annual Percentage Rate	6.90%	19.80%
ANNUAL PERCENTAGE RATE	6.90%	19.80%

SEND PAYMENTS TO: CITIBANK PREFERRED P.O. BOX 6001 THE LAKES, NV 88901-6001   5012N

Table 1: Statement /

08/09/95

	7/11
7/09	7/11
7/09	7/11
7/09	7/11
7/10	7/11
7/10	7/11
7/11	7/11
7/11	7/11
7/11	7/11
7/11	7/11

	Previous Balance	(+) Purchases & Advances	(–) Payments	(–) Credits	(+)FINANCE CHARGE	(+) Late Charges	(=) New Balance		
								Purchases Minimum Due	524.00
								Advances Minimum Due	
Purchases	24731.46	279.78			143.76		25155.00	Amount Over Credit Line	155.00
Advances								Fees / Past Due	515.00
Total	24731.46	279.78			143.76		25155.00	Minimum Amount Due	1194.00

Rate Summary Number of days this Billing Period 30	Purchases	Advances
Balance Subject to Finance Charge	25001.91	
Periodic Rate (Purchases-Monthly, Advances-Daily)	.57500%	.01890%
Nominal Annual Percentage Rate	6.90%	6.90%
ANNUAL PERCENTAGE RATE	6.90%	6.90%

SEND PAYMENTS TO: CITIBANK PREFERRED P.O. BOX 6100 THE LAKES, NV 88901-6100   6253N

Closing Date

Make check or money order payable in U.S. dollars on a U.S. bank to Citibank. Include account number on check or money order. No cash please.

obtained the 6.9 % percent interest. This interest rate is lower than Citibank allows consumers in a debt management organization. Creditors will not allow a consumer to use his credit card in a debt management program. This consumer was able to obtain a low interest rate and continue to use his credit card because he had a good payment history.

In 1995, a line of credit as high as shown was unheard of. In two short years, banks offer credit card limits to $100,000.

Consumers who have been carrying a balance for several years and have a good payment history can use this technique. *Do not mention a promotional interest rate.*

Creditors make more money off of you than any other customer because of the finance charges you pay. This technique to lower the interest rate works on a permanent basis and lets you keep your current credit card. When you call the creditor and speak to someone with authority, let that person know you have been a good-paying customer for a very long time. There is no reason why you should be paying high interest rates! *You deserve the maximum benefits because you are their best customer.*

Creditors will say that they do not lower the interest rate on past purchases. This is not true! The Citibank statement represents a perfect example. I have instructed consumers on negotiating lower interest rates on past and present purchases—in rare cases, cash advances. Odds are that somebody is paying your creditor a lower interest rate than you are. You want the creditor to know how important it is to you to continue to be a good-paying customer because you have a good credit file and you want to keep it that way, but you want and deserve relief in the form of a lower interest rate. If you do not get any results the first time, call back at a later date.

You can also give your credit card back to the creditor and obtain a good credit file. This technique deals more with rules than laws. In order to make it more successful, I recommend you do a budget. Refer to the sample letter at the end of this chapter (actual letters that were sent to creditors for consumers). In some cases we had to include a budget along with the letter. You can negotiate over the phone and mail your budget in, or do all your correspondence to the creditor through the mail.

These letters or phone calls can save you thousands of dollars in finance charges. Do not confuse this technique with the technique known as "Budget Option."

Lowering your interest rate works with department stores as well as banks.

When you give your credit card back to the creditor, your goal is to obtain the lowest interest rate possible. I have seen interest rates waived by creditors for consumers. Your interest rate is in writing on your monthly statement. If you look at your statement, you will see that the majority of the minimum monthly payment is interest. Sometimes the interest or finance charges make up *ninety percent* of the minimum monthly payment. The creditors want to keep you in hock. It's time to get out of hock.

Your goal is to have your interest rate lowered or waived. Do not let the creditor lower your monthly payment by just lowering your minimum due each month or you will be paying back the creditor forever and you will tarnish your credit report. Your only goal is to have your finance charges lowered or waived. If you want to retain a good credit file, continue to pay your required minimum monthly payment. Your minimum monthly payment will come down rapidly when no finance charges are added to your balance. Creditors want to hear good excuses. I am sure you can come up with one or you would not be carrying a balance.

The most common excuse in this particular situation is to tell the creditor you are over-burdened with debt and you want to do something about it before your debting situation deteriorates. This excuse is more than likely a fact or you would not be carrying a balance.

My opinion: the longer you have been a customer and the higher your interest rate, the more the creditor owes you, and please (for your benefit) do not tell the creditor what my opinion is. If you pay your minimum monthly payment required by your original credit card contract and make all your payments on time, the only mark you might have in your credit file is a statement above your account saying payment arrangement or something of that nature. This statement should be removed after you pay off your balance or close the account. The only difference you will see in your credit file after you close the account is a zero balance as long as you paid as agreed. The statement in your credit file is not that big of a deal.

If your objective is to obtain a good credit file, then you must make the minimum monthly payment required by your original credit card contract. I stress the importance of the subject because that is where consumers made mistakes—they don't make their minimum monthly payments. You can use the sample letter that follows—in or out of a debt management program.

More and more creditors are referring consumers to Consumer Credit Counseling Services. The majority of the consumers I know are in Genus Credit Management and have good credit files. They use the services for the benefit of waived or reduced finance charges. Refer to the sample letter earlier.

For You To Decide

If you're having trouble paying your unsecured payments including credit card payments and you're cutting back on clothing, food and needs for your children, you are making a mistake.

If all your property is exempt, there is no reason you should be working and living for your credit card creditors. Even in a Chapter 13 bankruptcy payment plan expense schedule, there is a space you fill in for *recreation*. You might be worried about damaging your credit report. Your credit report could already be damaged. The creditors want you to live for your credit report and work for them.

Over 60 percent of the credit reports have negative information.

In America, 10% of the households have a bankruptcy filing in their credit files.

If a credit report meant so much to employers, the unemployment rate would be sky high, not at 4.6% (the lowest unemployment rate since 1973). You need to make a strong character move. If you are working for your credit card creditors, you need to read this entire publication to help you decide what to do.

One option: do a budget and payment plan, then send it to each of your credit card creditors and other unsecured creditors. I will explain how to do a budget in this chapter under Budget Option.

If you live in a state with generous exceptions, you and your family are very fortunate. I feel especially sorry for consumers who live in states without generous exemptions. These consumers, not educated on personal finances, got caught up in the bank's free-wheeling credit card lending practices. Large credit card debt slowly but surely maxed-out credit cards, making the consumer work for the creditors. In other words, the banks' liberal credit card lending practices led to these large balances. If the banks would analyze these consumers' personal finances as they do for a home mortgage, this would not happen.

Freddie Mac (short for Federal Home Loan Mortgage Corp.) does not buy credit card paper. Freddie Mac provides a market to buy mortgages from lenders who meet their requirements. The banks are allowed an open house on credit card loans, like the billions of credit solicitations and pre-approved applications mailed out.

Look at these facts, example common among consumers who carry a balance on their credit cards:

- The consumer could have used that money paid in finance charges alone to pay cash for everything charged.

- The consumer (read that as you) could have paid cash for two of every item charged within a few years.

- The higher your interest rate and the longer you carry a balance, the more detrimental it is to your personal finance. In other words, you might be getting what you want now, but you could end up paying for it indefinitely. It can get even worse if you continue to charge purchases and carry balances on your credit cards.

- *Your debt is rising faster than your income.* When your debt payments match your income, you do not have any money left over to purchase anything else, much less do anything else. You end up working for your creditors. If you do not do anything about it now, you will be working for your credit card creditors the rest of your life. This will affect you not just financially but emotionally as well.

- If it were not for the bankruptcy laws that govern our great country, debtors would be without homes because the credit card creditors would take their homes in return for larger profits. This would definitely backfire on the creditors, and our government knows that.

- The bankruptcy laws keep the creditors intact. At the rate consumer bankruptcy is increasing, *in less than thirty years every other household in America will have filed bankruptcy.*

- The #1 cause consumers file bankruptcy is credit card debt. Consumer bankruptcy filings follow credit card delinquencies in the same pattern.

- The only way to control the creditors' credit card lending practices is to hit them in their pocketbooks, not by changing the bankruptcy laws to favor the banks. As I type these words, Congress debates bankruptcy bills. If these bills pass, they will reduce your rights as a debtor and it tears me up because of the big banks' control. I know the facts. If one of the bills in Congress passes to favor the big banks, you will see a surge of pre-approved credit card applications. The big banks will have the credit card debtor over the barrel. I have sent out over one hundred letters in favor of the consumer, but that is another story.

Some consumers do not understand why bankruptcies have reached record levels in 1997 while the economy is doing well. It has to do with the banks' credit card lending practices and the consumer. Not until the early part of 1994 did banks start slowing down on credit card loans. It takes several years for consumers to run up their credit cards and for their monthly expenses to start costing them more than they earn. Eventually some of these consumers end up discharging their credit card loans by filing bankruptcy. Bankruptcy filings will remain high until the effect of the banks' slowing down on making credit card loans is felt. The responsibility should rest on the bank's lending habits for a lot of reasons.

My personal beliefs about bankruptcy responsibility were completely different until I researched the facts. Large creditors such as commercial banks want the bankruptcy laws changed to favor the large profits they are already acquiring off of the average American consumer. The banks will use excuses like "Our good-paying customers are paying for the consumers who file bankruptcy." The banks have been overcharging the good-paying customer in credit card finance charges and hidden fees for three decades. Banks will continue to overcharge the good-paying customer, no matter what the credit card loan delinquency rate is. If bankruptcy laws change to favor big banks, the only pockets that will grow are the big banks'.

In the past, the return on credit card assets was almost *four times* the return compared to other banking activities. Creditors have made a huge profit margin on credit card loans and they want more. These words came from a high-ranking banking executive:

"I have no loyalty to my bank—all that matters to them is larger profits. If the bank could, they would dissolve my position in order to obtain larger profits."

The banks complain about the $9 billion credit card loan losses from bankruptcy filings in 1997. The banks fail to mention the billions and billions more they made off the same consumers in past years who discharged their credit card loans in bankruptcy in 1997. A lot of these same consumers now discharging their credit card loans in bankruptcy carried balances for 10 years, 15 years, and longer. Throughout those years the banks made more than enough in profits of these consumers in finance charges to make up for the balances that these consumers discharged in bankruptcy. In the majority of these cases the banks will make a larger profit off the consumer who discharged his debt in bankruptcy than they will the life of a good-paying credit card customer. The good-paying costumer will not pay in as much in finance charges compared to the bankruptcy consumer.

Do not feel too bad for the banks: their profits for 1997 are close to $60 billion! It was another year of record-breaking profits for the banks.

Why credit card debt can be bad debt, no matter what interest rate you're paying.

Some consumers use their credit cards for business purposes. I know of an individual who took out cash advances on several different credit cards. Then he joined a debt management program to reduce his average interest rate from approximately 18% down to an average of 7% on all his credit cards.

He used the money to purchase a home as *an investment*. He saved money on closing costs and interest rates by using his credit cards. He paid off the credit card balances after he sold the property for a large profit. With the home insured, little chance existed for the creditors to lose their money. Your credit card account should have some history before your interest rates are reduced or waived. I would never recommend a consumer to use credit card debt to finance any speculative business ventures such as investing in someone else's business or a start-up business.

Why credit card debt can be bad debt.

Credit card debt can be bad debt because"

- The items you charge on a credit cards usually depreciate faster than any other property you own. Most items purchased on a credit card have a zero return value after purchase.

- You will never see a return on your money. Even if your credit cards were interest-free, you would still pile up debt by charging and carrying a balance (on zero return items). To the best of your ability you should pay cash for zero return items or purchases you will never see a return for, like clothing and dining out.

- When have you ever recouped any return on items you purchased with a credit card? When you sell a vehicle financed several years ago, money is left over after the loan pay-off. When have you ever sold the same items you purchased on credit and then paid off your credit card balances? Even if you tried to sell the items you purchased on credit in a garage sale, you might recoup a few hundred dollars to pay down the balance on your credit cards. You would still owe thousands.

- The American consumer is paying an average of 17% interest on plastic. If you are in the middle of the road federal income tax bracket, you would have to make a 24% return on and investment that equaled your total credit card balances in order to break even. The ten-year average return of the stock market is 15.9%. The return in the stock market is not guaranteed. The average consumer who is in the middle of the road federal income tax bracket is required to pay 24% on credit card balances.

- If you default on your credit card loan, the creditor wants to take your home, retirement plan, or any other property that is more valuable than all the stuff you purchased on your credit cards like clothes, television, and other fat items that you charged. The creditors want the protein in exchange for the fat. If the law allowed it, the creditors would take all your protein items, in exchange for all your fat items.

A debtor is a consumer who uses credit card loans, owes money on a personal loan, or is paying on a home mortgage. For example, I have a friend who has never been a debtor. He has never financed a purchase in his life, including his home. He has never made a budget in his life. The more debt you have, the more budgets or budgeting you must do. More-debt, more-paperwork, more-headaches. Ask Donald Trump.

I want to share with you one more thing before we move into "budget option." I have a disease called *spendalitis*. I have a spending problem. I have to pay cash for everything. What I do not spend, I give away. I think I was born with this disease. The good thing about having spendalitis is that a remedy for it exists. Not a person in this world has an allergy to this remedy. The remedy is called *debt-free*. Like any remedy, it takes time for you to feel the full impact of it.

If you have spendalitis or not, the same philosophy applies. You should pay cash for zero return items and finance protein items only. Financing a protein item like a home is fine, and one fat item like a car is okay too. But if you finance a car, boat, a camper and a motorcycle, then you have way too much fat in your finances. You will feel the fat in your finances. It will feel worse than being a thousand pounds overweight. If you have that much fat in your finances, you know exactly what I am talking about.

Budget Option — Bankruptcy Is Not For Me!

Always let the creditor know what your plans are, what you plan on paying them each month or if you do not plan on paying them at all. You are doing yourself a favor when you let the creditors know what your plans are. The bank's credit card employees rare among the easiest people to deal with in the credit industry because they are employees just like you.

Some credit card creditors will let you charge off the account by asking them to, and stop adding finance charges and late fees to your account. Sometime in the future, you might pay it off. If the creditor stops adding finance charges and late fees, you would save some money down the road.

A charge-off usually occurs after the account has not had any activity for six months or longer. Some creditors will just hold it as a collection account. The big banks have been backing off this approach, driving the consumer into bankruptcy for several reasons:

- Once the debt is erased in bankruptcy, the banks will never see any money.

- Millions of consumers are discharging their credit card debt in bankruptcy.

- Pressure from consumer advocate groups and Washington because of the high consumer bankruptcy rate.

As I type this sentence, bankruptcy debates go on in Washington.

Here's the way it works. You get bad marks in your credit file for not paying as agreed. You can protect yourself under the law without filing bankruptcy. Because consumers over-burdened with credit card debt and with personal reasons did not want to file bankruptcy, they asked me what to do. So I wrote the chapter on "budget option."

I did not write this book, *Debt Control,* to tell you how to spend your money. I will leave that up to you. I told you how I stay out of debt. I will give you advice on getting the most out of your income when using this kind of budget. I wrote *Debt Control* to show you how to stop working for your credit card creditors and start working for yourself. Books, software, church support groups and several other sources can explain how to budget your money. The budget ideas I propose to you help you take advantage of the laws that govern our great country, the bankruptcy laws for consumers overburdened with debt.

Having protection under the law does not mean using the law; you do not have to file bankruptcy. If you follow the guidelines in budget option, why would the big banks drive you, an honest consumer, into court? If they do, you will go to court with the evidence to support your case. The big banks, the "fat cats," are not out in the public dealing with consuming Americans over their heads because of credit card debt like I have been. These are people who have been for five, ten, fifteen, twenty years, living and working for their credit card creditors. The majority of these consumers, honest hard-working Americans, need a second chance.

If you just ran up a bunch of credit cards illegitimately in the last year, you can put this book away. Besides, the banks and bankruptcy judges are smarter than that.

Fat cats do not include any employees of the Federal Reserve. The Federal Reserve is working for America as hard—or harder than—any other government affiliate.

The following budget was designed for the average consumer, the consumer who does not have a lot of assets. Anyone over-burdened with credit card debt can use it. You can hire a professional to help you, like an experienced Chapter 13 bankruptcy attorney or one of his associates.

If your budget is more complex such as a rental property, small business or other non-exempt property, professional help represents an excellent alternative. Whenever you hire a professional for services, get the total cost in writing. It is important for you and other people to know that you care about your money.

If you do not want to file bankruptcy and the budget option is not for you, find an *attorney* experienced at negotiating with creditors. Use your Yellow Pages to shop around. Do not attempt to negotiate partial repayments to creditors on your own.

"Budget Option" is a full repayment plan.

If you know that you are going to make your own monthly budget, read the rest of this book, then come back to do your budget. Nobody is going to see your first budget but you unless you need a friend to help you. You have to be totally honest. If you're not totally honest, you will have to come back and start over.

Do not get stressed out doing your budget. You are in control if you want to be. It is time to take control. Get a calculator and a piece of notebook paper. Draw a line down the middle of the notebook paper. On the top left side of the notebook paper write **Income**. On the top right side, write **Expenses**.

Income, expenses and deductions are all averaged monthly. Every set of numbers you write down on the notebook paper will be *monthly averages* of your yearly total. For example, if your take-home pay is $40,000 a year, divide that by 12 months.

If you get paid *weekly*, multiply that by 4.3 (that is the number of weeks in a month). For example, $420 x 4.3 = $1806.

If you get paid *biweekly*, multiply that by 2.16. For example $840 x 2.16 = 1814.

Use the same formula for all deductions that came out of your paycheck. You can use your last two paycheck stubs. Use your paycheck stubs to figure everything on a *monthly average* of your yearly total. If your income fluctuates because of commissions or overtime, estimate your monthly average. If you estimate your income to be the same this year as last year, use the last paycheck stub you received in December, of last year, then multiply everything by 12. If you use your W-2, make sure you do not forget any deduction that came out of your paycheck.

Under the income column on your notebook paper, write down your gross pay and every deduction that came out of your paycheck to get your net pay or take-home pay. This includes taxes, social security, savings plans (401K), medical, dental or any other deduction that came out of your paycheck. The left side of the notebook paper should look just like your check stub, except everything is based on a monthly average of your yearly total.

If you have other income besides your take-home pay— spouse earnings, child support and any other income that your household receives—include it as well. After all your income and deduction are accounted for, you should have a good estimate of your total monthly take-home pay or total monthly income. You total monthly income is the figure you will use to subtract your total monthly expenses from.

Time to do **expenses**. Do not include any expenses like credit card payments or other unsecured debt that can be discharged in bankruptcy. You will write this type of debt on your *payment plan*, not your budget. Write everything down on the right side of the notebook paper under **Expenses**. You will average your expenses just like income on a monthly average of your yearly total. For example, if your auto insurance costs you $750 every six months you will divide 750 by 6 or 750 ÷ 6 = $125 for your monthly average of your yearly total. You will include priority payments, secured loans, mortgage or rent, auto payments, life insurance, health insurances, student loans, child support, etc. Payments that you make to creditors must be written down to the exact dollar amount of the monthly payment. You ask why? Every creditor that you send your budget to will pull your credit report to verify your budget. Each of the creditors will want to make sure that they are being treated fairly.

At the end of this chapter, you will find a **Chapter 13 Expense Schedule J**. Use it as a guide when doing your expenses. You might have to add categories that the following budget does not have, such as dining out (fast foods), personal care, cigarettes, child care and other items. You will have to estimate items such as transportation expenses (not car payments), clothes, utilities, medical and dental expenses (do not include medical and dental insurance).

If you estimate $500 a year on clothing, then divide 500 by 12 or 500 ÷ 12 = 42 a month. Do not include any expenses you subtract from your income. You should now have a total of your monthly expenses.

Subtract you monthly expenses from your monthly income. You will have what is called *excess income*. Write your excess income on the bottom of the notebook paper. Each of your credit card creditors and other unsecured creditors would get their share of this excess income in a Chapter 13 payment plan for 36 to 60 months.

In a Chapter 13 expense schedule, you do not add cigarettes or dining out. You could try working those items in somewhere. You could use what I call *budget transfers* for a Chapter 13 as well. Your attorney would guide you if she though you over-did it in categories like recreation. We do not care about that because you are not filing bankruptcy. You are making a different commitment with your creditors: you are not discharged any of your debts. In a Chapter 13 bankruptcy, the average debtor usually discharges a large portion of his debts. You are going to take care of yourself and family. That is what budget transfers are all about.

Budget Transfers

How much excess income do you have left? If you are like most consumers—overburdened with credit card debt—you have a figure from 60% to 70% of the total you pay your unsecured creditors. If you have $1000 a month in credit card payments, you should have approximately $650 in excess income. The higher your finance charges, the more excess income you will have. In some cases, you might have less than average excess income.

Remember, the only person who will see this budget is you. You will be making legitimate budget transfers. Take that excess income and apply it to expenses that you need, and expenses that are important to you.

The following represent legitimate budget transfers:

- When was the last time you or the kids went to the dentist? Increase medical or dental expenses.

- Car repairs. When you need them, you need them now. They are expensive. Does your car need new tires, transmission or something else? Increase transportation expenses. Transportation expenses are usually high; it is expensive to maintain an automobile, provide gasoline, oil, dealer maintenance and other things.

- You and your children need some new clothing. Buy some this coming year. Increase your clothing expense.

- You might want to start a diet, but eating fat-free food is expensive. Increase your food bill.

- You want a membership at a health club to get fit. Get one. You have a better reason than a consumer who filed bankruptcy to increase your recreation activities. Even though your not filing bankruptcy, you do not want to get carried away on categories like recreation. Joining a health club would be personal care to me.

- You have been wanting to give more to the church, but your credit card payments have been holding you back. Not anymore. Increase charitable contributions.

- If your credit report is still in good standing and you need a new car, buy one while you can obtain financing at a reasonable rate. This is legal. Make sure you add it to your budget under expenses so that all your creditors know.

I am sure you get it by now. You can start working for yourself and family without filing bankruptcy. Your budget makes it work. You do not have to keep all your receipts every time you buy something; nobody is going to ask for them. Some consumers keep all their receipts so they know exactly where their money went. I used to keep all my receipts.

Karen had $900 a month in credit card payments. She had $600 a month in excess income. I asked her what she wanted to do more than anything. She said to put her little girl in a private school. I said, do it. Karen lived in town. The neighborhood is a little rough. We worked her excess income down to $110. I know a consumer paying as little as $50 a month and owing $40,000 to seven different creditors.

You're thinking, "My credit card creditors are going to sue me." The truth is, they will be thrilled to death you are paying in something and you did not file bankruptcy. They just won't tell you. You credit rating will sink to the bottom of the sea. Usually the banks are content with that (read Chapter Four for bad credit advice). Just as bankruptcy consumers can rebuild credit, you can too. It will be hard for you to get an unsecured credit card. If that is what got you in the hole in the first place, who needs it?

You're thinking, "I will be paying my credit card creditor forever." No, you won't. Eventually, your creditors will stop adding finance chargers at some point. Do not be surprised if they stop adding finance charges and late fees the day they receive your budget, payment plan and Sample letter #2. When your personal finances improve, you can increase your monthly payment plan, but only if you think your budget allows it.

Now go back and *redo the budget*. This is the one you will be sending to all your creditors who will be in your monthly payment plan. *Make sure you come up with a budget you can live with, not one your credit card creditors or a debt management program wants you to live by.*

You send this budget only to the creditors in your monthly payment plan. You do not send it to your secured creditors. You will pay your secured and priority creditors as agreed.

You will have to trash every credit card you have. Get a Visa or MasterCard debt card, or secured credit card. You must include every single unsecured creditor who is on your credit report in this payment plan. The majority of the consumers I know were thrilled to death that they were trashing all their credit cards. After reading this Chapter, you might be thrilled, too.

Budget Option- Your "Payment Plan"

We will make a *payment plan* by splitting up your excess income. Each unsecured creditor will receive their portion of your excess income. It must be split up fairly. You have to give each creditor a percentage of your excess income. We will use Karen's excess income as an example. She had a $110 left to split up between five credit card creditors. You will add up the total you owe all your creditors who were not included in your budget. In the payment plan example I am using here, the total owed all five creditors comes to $20,000. Karen owed more than $20,000!Payment Plan Example

This is the formula:

Amount owed to each of the five creditors:
6,257 + 5,143 + 4,170 + 2,332 + 2,098 = 20,000.
Divide amount owed to each creditor by 20,000.
For example, Citibank 6,257 ÷ 20,000 = 31.2.
Round off fractions, 31.2% to the closest whole number.

The closest whole number is 31%. The closest whole number to 25.7% is 26%.

Multiply .31 (the percentage) by your excess income. For example, .31 x 110 = 34.10. Citibank will receive $34.10 per month. First Card will receive $28.60 per month. Discover will receive $23.10 per month, Sears $13.30 per month and Chase $11.00 per month.

Monthly Payment Plan

Account	Formula	Amount Owed
Citibank	$6,257 ÷ 20,000 =31.2%. Round it off to 31% x 110	$ 34.10
First Card	$5,143 ÷ 20,000 = 25.7% Round it off to 26% x 110	$ 28.60
Discover	$4,170 ÷ 20,000 = 20.8% Round it off to 21% x 110	$ 23.10
Sears	$2,332 ÷20,000 = 11.6% Round it off to 12% x 110	$ 13.20
Chase	$2,098 ÷20,000 = 10.4% Round it off to 10% x 110	$ 11.00
Total	Karen's Excess Income	$110.00

Along with your budget, you will send a copy of your payment plan—just like the one above—to each of your unsecured creditors.

Where are the non-profit organizations when you need them? They are working for the creditors. No debt management organization will fund your payment plan because it is not 60% to 80%

of what your monthly payments were. It is 10% of your original monthly payments.

Now I will show you how to *fund the plan* without writing five different checks each month. You set up *direct withdrawals* for each creditor out of your checking account. You can set it up where each creditor gets paid automatically. Every month their payments will automatically be drafted out of your checking account. This is one of the privileges of having a checking account. All you have to do is make sure you have enough in your checking account to cover the direct withdrawal. Do not forget to empty accounts at banks who are included in your payment plan, because if you don't, they will. You might have to open a new checking account.

If you have a good personal relationship with a bank, you might not want to include them in your payment plan. You have other options. Turn the loan into a secured loan, or you can pay off the unsecured loan.

If you do not feel comfortable about your small monthly payments to each creditor, do not take my word for it. Go visit a Chapter 13 bankruptcy attorney for reassurance. Do not tell him you are not going to file bankruptcy. He might try to talk you into it. Consumers go to bankruptcy attorneys with credit card debt as the only problem and end up filing bankruptcy. There is no law saying you have to file bankruptcy. Thanks to the bankruptcy laws, dischargeable debt is negotiable debt. That is why this payment plan is possible.

More On Budget Option

You must be committed to repaying your creditors in full. If you do mathematical estimates, you will discover that it will not take as long as you think to pay back your creditors in full. Consumers take out home equity loans for ten, fifteen and twenty years to pay off credit card balances. *Remember, finance charges eat up a large portion of your monthly payments.* The creditors should eliminate your finance charges after they receive your budget.

You must be committed to adding no more debt—credit card or other unsecured debt—to your personal finances. This does not mean you cannot use a plastic card such as *one* charge card or secured credit card or debt card, or get a loan for medical emergencies, secured loans, a gas card, auto loan, or home financing.

The statute of limitations does not mean anything to you. You are renewing a commitment.

The creditors will be monitoring your credit report. In some states, even deed transactions are reported in a consumer's credit file. It is a good ideal to obtain copies of your credit reports.

Your finances are not under court supervision as in Chapter 13 bankruptcy. The bankruptcy trustee or debt management program will not take their cut out of your monthly payment. This is good for the creditors. You are in control if you what to be.

As your financial situation improves, you can send surplus checks to each creditor that is included in your payment plan. You must treat each creditor in your payment plan fairly.

From my experience, it is impossible to qualify for a "standard mortgage" when charge-offs or collection accounts are in your credit file. There are other types of mortgages available, but you will have to pay for them in finance charges. However, other alternatives exist in real estate.

In some cases you might have to explain your budget and payment plan when applying for a mortgage or credit. If you have a relationship with a bank, you might be able to obtain low finance charges on a collateralized loan or an auto loan.

You reorganized your finances without filing bankruptcy. Refer to sample letter #2 at the end of the chapter.

Expense Schedule

Use this Expense Schedule to help you figure your expenses. This is the same expense schedule used for a Chapter 13 Bankruptcy Budget. An actual budget example follows this form where the numbers are filled in.

Rent or home mortgage payments .... $_____
Are real estate taxes included? .... Yes __ No __
Is property insurance included? .... Yes __ No __
Utilities, Electricity and heating fuel .... $_____
Water and sewer... $_____
Telephone .... $_____
Cable .... $_____
Other (type of utilities)... $_____
Home maintenance (repairs and upkeep)...................................... $_____
Food (I eat heavy.) .... $_____
Clothing.. $_____
Laundry and dry cleaning .... $_____
Medical and dental expenses (not insurance)................................ $_____
Transportation (not including car payments)................................. $_____
Children Activities .... $_____
Recreation clubs (do not get carried away.)................................... $_____
Entertainment (do not get carried away.)....................................... $_____
Newspapers .... $_____
Magazines etc. .... $_____
Charitable contributions... $_____
Insurance
        (not deducted from wages or included in home mortgage payments)...... $_____
Insurance-Homeowner's or renter's .... $_____
Insurance-Life .... $_____
Insurance-Health... $_____
Insurance-Auto .... $_____
Insurance-Other (type)... $_____
Taxes (not deducted from wages or included in home mortgage payments. Specify the
        type of taxes (i.e., property taxes).
Type.. $_____
Installment payments: .... $_____
Auto (total of all auto loans).. $_____
Other installment loan.. $_____
Alimony, maintenance, and support to others................................. $_____
Payments for support of additional dependents not living at your home.......... $_____
Professional expenses .... $_____
One of the benefits of this budget: you are not filing bankruptcy.
        Personal care (I added this one.).. $_____
        Dining out (I added this one. Do not get carried away)........................ $_____
        You add one .... $_____
TOTAL MONTHLY EXPENSES .... $_____
TOTAL MONTHLY NET INCOME... $_____
EXCESS INCOME .... $_____
This is the total amount to be split up between the credits included in your payment plan.
In our payment plan example, the excess income was $110.

Schedule J (Budget) Expenses

Rent or Home Mortgage Payment (include job rented for mobile home)	$ 1350.00
Are real estate taxes included?　　　Yes　　No	
Is property insurance included?　　　Yes　　No	
Utilities: Electricity and heating fuel	$ 200.00
Water and sewer	$ 60.00
Telephone	$ 95.00
Other — Natural Gas	$ 25.00
Other — Cable	$ 48.00
Other —	$ 0.00
Home maintenance (repairs & upkeep)	$ 25.00
Food	$ 400.00
Clothing	$ 50.00
Laundry and Dry Cleaning	$ 39.00
Medical & Dental expenses	$ 50.00
Transportation (not including car payments)	$ 200.00
Recreation, clubs, and entertainment, newspapers, magazines, etc...	$ 45.00
Charitable contributions	$ 40.00
Insurance (not deducted from wages or included in home mortgage payments)	
Homeowner's or renter's	$ 0.00
Life	$ 30.00
Health	$ 80.00
Auto	$ 150.00
Other — House Insurance	$ 150.00
Other —	$ 0.00
Taxes (not deducted from wages or included in home mortgage payments)	

Schedule J (Budget) Expenses

Specific — Property Taxes	$ 500.00
Installment payments (in chapter 12 & 13 cases, do not list payments to be included)	
Auto	$1,000.00
Other —	$ 0.00
Alimony, maintenance, and support paid to others	$ 0.00
Payments for support of additional dependents not living at your home	$ 0.00
Regular expenses from operation of business, profession or farm (attach detail statement)	$0.00
Other — WD	$ 600.00
Other —	$ 0.00
TOTAL MONTHLY EXPENSES (Summary of Schedule)	$ 5,117.00

A. Total projected monthly income	$ 5,312.39
B. Total projected monthly expenses	$ 5,117.00
C. Excess Income (A minus B)	$ 195.39
D. Total amount to be paid into plan each — Monthly	$ 195.00

The excess income on this sample budget that will be divided among unsecured creditors is $195.00.

Sample Letter #1.

This is not the letter for budget option—use the next sample letter.

Name Of Creditor
Department The Letter Is Going To
Mailing Address
City, State And Zip

Your Name
Address
City, State And Zip
Your Account # 0000-0000-0000-0000

I am burdened with debt. I understand I have other options but retaining a good credit file is important to me. I have been a good paying customer for a long time. I am doing something about it before my financial situation deteriorates and I have to seek relief. I will continue to pay my minimum monthly payment as agreed in my original credit card contract. I am looking for relief in the elimination of my finance charges. In return, I will forfeit my credit card. If my finances improve, I will inform (Name Of Creditor). I have enclosed a budget to back up my claim.

Regretfully yours,

Your Signature
(Print Your Name)

For several reasons, this technique does not carry the clout that Budget Option does. One reason is your credit report. If you want to retain a good credit report, the banks make you pay for it in finance charges. At least you are trashing the credit card. You can print or type this letter. When you do your budget like I explain in Budget Option, make sure you include all your creditors as part of your expenses. This includes your credit card creditors as well. I am sure you understand that your expenses must be more than your income. In other words, you have no excess income (Income minus expenses = excess income). Do not send a payment plan in when doing this type of budget. Send a budget only to the creditors you want to forfeit your credit cards to. More than likely, it will be the credit cards with the highest finance charges. You do not have to forfeit all your credit cards when using this letter. Do not get this confused with Budget Option.

Sample Letter #2

For Budget And Payment Plan.

Name Of Creditor
Department The Letter Is Going To
Mailing Address
City, State And Zip.

Your Name
Address
City, State and Zip
Your Account # 0000-0000-0000-0000

I am over-burdened with debt. Due to my personal financial situation, I am a candidate for bankruptcy. I do not want to file bankruptcy like millions of other consumers. I chose to pay back my creditors in full for the principal. In return, I am asking you to immediately stop adding finance charges and late fees. I understand that charging my account-off will have and adverse effect on my credit report for seven years from the date of the original late payment or charge-off. I have enclosed my budget and payment plan. I structured it like a Chapter 13 bankruptcy. When my excess income increases, I will increase my payments into my plan.

Regretfully yours,

Your Signature
(Print Your Name)

You can print or type your budget, payment plan and letter. Your letter might not look exactly like this. Depending how far behind you are on your payments. You do not need a response from the creditor. If it makes you feel better, you can ask for a response from the creditor. As long as you make your payments on time. Your budget, payment plan, commitment to repay and stay away from unsecured credit will hold up in court. The creditors know this too.

9

Dealing With Creditors And Collectors: Bankruptcy, Wait And See

If you decide to follow the guidelines in budget option, the majority of this chapter will not be necessary for you.

The Internal Revenue Service is the king of all creditors and collectors, we all know what powers the IRS has. Income taxes are a priority debt. If you are having problems with the Internal Revenue Service, I strongly suggest using a tax professional like a C.P.A. or tax attorney.

If your finances are limited, consult one of the several publications on how to deal with the Internal Revenue Service at your local book store or library. The best advice I can give you when dealing with the IRS is to learn before you launch. Consumers will meet with an IRS representative unprepared and then be intimidated, so it does not take much effort for an IRS representative to control them emotionally when they're scared. The IRS representatives will act according to the guidelines they are instructed to follow. Knowledge will give you confidence. The more knowledge you have, the more confidence you will have.

When you acquire enough knowledge, it's like taking a tax professional with you. However, knowledge takes time. Never meet with an Internal Revenue Service Representative unprepared.

The IRS will work with consumers who have very little income and property. You could possibly make an *Offer in Compromise*.

Concealing property from creditors is one thing but do not attempt to conceal property from the IRS.[1] Federal income taxes are what finance America and enable a debtor to receive the benefits allowed by law. In some cases, a debtor can even discharge federal income taxes. You should take the maximum tax deductions allowed and pay your federal income taxes to the best of your ability.

The auditors and collectors that work for the Internal Revenue Service actually work *for* you and me. The collectors I am referring to in this publication are working *against* you.

With the options available (and because of the laws that govern the American consumer), a consumer with a large dischargeable debt load should not have accounts that go to a collection agency or even have to hassle with the original creditor. However, not everyone thinks like me.

Do not let creditors or collectors control you emotionally. They might say things like, "It's your moral obligation to pay your debts." The only thing that you're morally obligated to is taking care of yourself and your family. The creditor took the risk and loaned you the money. How many times have you taken risk and it did not pan out?

If you do what you think should be done, the worst thing that will happen to you for not paying your debts is a bad credit report. A bad credit report can be repaired.

Always pay for your essentials first. Essentials include your mortgage or rent, children's needs, groceries, utility bills, insurance, clothing, car note or any other type of transportation you have to fund, child support payments, taxes and any other priority payments. After you pay for your essentials and priorities (if there is any money left over), pay your unsecured creditors, including credit or charge cards, medical bills, personal loans and any other unsecured debt payments that are not a priority. These types of

---

1 Some of you might throw this presentation out the window when I give you my opinion on income taxes. I said earlier that no place in the world is better to be in than in the United States of America when you are in debt. Some countries will cut a finger off; other countries will spread your name among the population. Of course, these tactics are illegal in our great country.

unsecured creditors are paid last. Do not let a creditor or collector talk you out of money you need to support yourself and your family.

Never write a hot check or a post-dated check to a creditor, collector or any business for that matter. When you write a hot check, you are a criminal. You are not a criminal when you do not pay your debts. You are classified as a debtor that did not pay as agreed. Even though you write a post-dated check in good faith, you are gambling. The funds might not be available as you expected. You should not write post-dated checks. The only exception to this rule: when you write a post-dated check to a friend or family member (because you have control over the check being cashed).

Each consumer's debt situation varies greatly due to several factors which I will list. The final decision on how to manage your debt rests entirely with you. You can take control of this situation (remember—creditors know you have other options like bankruptcy).

In a Chapter 7 bankruptcy, creditors receive nothing for "dischargeable" unsecured debt. You might not be successful on your first negotiation but do not give up.

Debtors unable to make their payments should contact their creditor and try to negotiate a voluntary repayment plan. If you were not successful at negotiating a payment that fits your budget with the original creditor, your delinquent account will be sent to the in-house collection department. You will have a second opportunity to work out a payment plan to fit your budget. Do not pay any more than you can afford, even if it is thirty dollars a month. If the creditor's collection department orally rejects your thirty dollars a month and that is all you can afford, send in the thirty dollars a month anyway and keep records of your payment. Pay every month on time. If and when your financial situation progresses, you can increase your monthly payment. This could save your account from going to a collection agency or even a lawsuit.

If your debt problem resembles the one described in chapter eight and you followed the guidelines in "budget option," you should not have to worry about being hassled. If you are bothered, follow the guidelines from these examples:

1. **If you do not want to file bankruptcy due to personal circumstances and the creditor rejects your thirty dollars a month and sues you.** Answer your summons and prepare yourself for your day in court. If you cannot afford an attorney, go to the public library and read one of several publications on representing yourself in court. In a situation like this, there is something better than having an attorney and using the public library when going to court. That something better is *evidence* to support your claim. Even an attorney would have a hard time representing you without evidence. The more evidence you have, the stronger your case will be. Evidence includes records describing your budget and property, your payment plan, commitment to repaying all your debts, pay stubs, rent or mortgage receipts, credit reports, all correspondence with the creditor and collector, all payment records associated with this account, and any other evidence associated with your personal fiances that will support your case. With this much evidence, you might be better off without an attorney. You must be committed to not acquiring new unsecured debt and to paying to the best of your ability. This does not mean you have to be living like a miser and moving into a one bedroom apartment, or selling off your exempt property. Remember that your unsecured creditors had no right to your exempt property to start with. I have sat in court to watch consumers back up their budgets and claims. Everybody wants to tell the judge a story. All I every hear the judge ask for is evidence. Judges want evidence, not stories. That goes for attorneys, too. I have seen attorneys try to get by with stories. The courts are open to the public: go see for yourself.

2. **Even after you're sued**, you can still continue to negotiate your collection account. You might reach a settlement and the creditor or collector will drop the lawsuit. Regardless of your personal financial situation—the worst thing you can do is nothing! The consumers I know who have hidden from their creditors in the past admit this prevented them from developing their financial potential. It was not until they cleared up their judgments and collection accounts (usually through bankruptcy) that they moved forward financially.

3. **Garnished Wages.** Having wages garnished is one of the most humiliating things that can happen to a consumer. First the creditor has to file a lawsuit against the consumer and obtain a judgment before wages can be garnished. *Do not hide from your creditors.*

4. **You encounter a professional collection agency.** If you were not able to work out a payment plan with the original creditors in-house collection department (or you just completely ignored all correspondence from the original creditor), your account is over four months delinquent and your credit rating is shot, your delinquent account likely will be sent off to a professional collection agency, passed on to a attorney, or sent to a separate company owned by the original creditor that is a collection agency. The law known as the *Fair Debt Collection Practices Act* applies to all three types of *collectors* hired by the original creditor that you owe. The Fair Debt Collection Practices Act *does not apply to the original creditor.* State laws can be stricter and apply to the original creditor as well as the collector.

In back of the book, you will find a public document called **Fair Debt Collection** to use as a guideline when dealing with collectors.

5. **Order creditors to stop calling**. You can use the second most-hated weapon allowed by law against a collector by immediately writing the collection agency a certified letter return receipt requested. Simply state that you want all communication to immediately stop. You do not have to worry about a collector pressuring you for money and information. The disadvantage to this letter: the next time you hear from the collector, it will be the last time, unless the creditor and collector decide to sue you. After you send your certified letter asking the collection agency to stop all communication and the collector continues to call you, ask your local phone company to monitor your incoming calls. The local phone company can identify who's calling you, even if your caller ID identifies the number as being unavailable. This would be an excellent source of evidence against the collection agency.

6. **If you decide to negotiate with a collection agency.** I recommend that you do it by corresponding through the mail and make copies of all outgoing letters. When you write your first letter to the collection agency, inform them that you will be negotiating through the mail *only* and that your employer does not allow collection agencies to call you at work. Collectors are professional

125

phone negotiators. Remember that you do not have to do what they ask you to do, orally or in writing. *You* can ask all the questions and not have to answer any questions.

7. **If you decide to negotiate over the telephone**. I advise you to record all conversations. You must follow the Federal Communications Commission laws that govern recording telephone conversations and local laws. The collector will watch his P's and Q's. And you will be able to use this as a reference source helping you to remember everything you told the collector. For several reasons, I strongly recommend you do all your negotiations through the mail. If you are negotiating for a dischargeable debt, remember that this debt can be erased in bankruptcy. Make absolutely sure it is a dischargeable debt. You must be familiar with your exempt property when using bankruptcy as a negotiation tool. *Only your exempt property is protected from creditors.* Bankruptcy can be your most powerful negotiating tool. Bankruptcy is a serious legal process. Do not throw the word around. You might be able to negotiate a settlement that makes more economic sense to your personal financial situation than bankruptcy. You can always try bypassing the collector and calling the creditor back to see if they will take the collection account back in order to make a settlement with you. Sometimes your collection or charge-off accounts are sold to collection agencies. If your account is sold to a collection agencies, you can forget about asking the creditor to take the account back. Note that your account was sold to a collection agency at a *discount*. The creditor might not have discounted your account, but the collection agency will. Some of these collection agencies pay pennies on the dollar for old charge-off accounts.

A *professional collector* is very friendly and kind. This type of collector can do more damage to you than an inexperienced, rude collector. Collectors use several different techniques to collect accounts. *All a collector wants is your money.*

Do not tell a collector anything about your personal finance. If you are trying to negotiate a lower lump sum payment for your collection account and the collector knows where you are getting the money from, the collector will want more money from you.

If a collector asks you where the funds are coming from, answer politely, "None of your business." The collector does not make the actual decision on filing a lawsuit against the consumer;

the original creditor makes that decision. The collection agency will affect the decision whether a lawsuit will be filed or not. Everything you tell the collector or creditor will be factored into the lawsuit decision. You might be better off not even talking to a creditor or collector until you know exactly what you are going to do. *The only thing a collector wants from you is your money. The last thing the creditor wants to do is file a lawsuit against you.*

Both the creditor and collector want something from you. Most consumers do not realize how much in control of the situation they really are. Lawsuits are expensive and take time. Is the debt you owe worth pursuing by the creditor? What does your current credit report tell them about you? Are you gainfully employed? What did you tell them about yourself? Do you maintain a stable residence? What are your state exemptions? Is your checking account still active? How old is the collection account? Are you judgment-proof? You could have them believing that you are judgment-proof. These are questions the creditor and collector will use to determine if the lawsuit is beneficial to the creditor. Creditors obtaining a judgement against a debtor in Texas cannot garnish hourly or salary wages.

In Texas, some consumers walked away from their debt that could be discharged in bankruptcy and were not sued by the creditor before the statute of limitations expired.

I will give you a few of the reasons why you might not want to walk away from your debt.

1. You might have it on your conscience from three to ten years, (depending on what state you live in) for the statute of limitations to expire. In Texas, the statute of limitations runs four years for contracts, notes and open accounts.

2. It would be very difficult to reestablish credit having several collection accounts in your credit file. If you wanted to obtain a standard mortgage, you would have to pay these collection accounts off, wait until the statue of limitations expired or wait for seven years for the collection accounts to come off your credit file.

3. If it is a joint account, the creditor can come after the other account holder, like your spouse.

Judgment-proof means your income and property remain exempt from creditors. Refer to your state exemptions to see what is exempt from a judgment in your state. Most judgment-proof consumers have very little income and property or have concealed their income and property. Refer to Exempt Property at the back of the book to learn how to obtain your state exemptions.

Use your state exemptions to know what wages and property are exempt from creditors if they obtained a judgment against you. If creditors obtain a judgment against you, they usually go after your wages first. In a few states even your wages cannot be garnished. In the states where your wages cannot be garnished, your savings and checking accounts in your name are not protected. If your savings rest in a retirement plan and it is exempt property in your state, then it is protected from creditors. Remember that these laws which protect your wages from garnishment do *not* apply to delinquent federal taxes, child support and government-guaranteed student loans.

If you live in a state where your wages cannot be garnished, the creditor sues you and wins a judgment against you. Then you could live on a *cash basis*, have someone write your checks for you and use an authorized credit card. Some consumers could try getting away with this (depending on their exempt property and support from sources like family and friends). Example: putting contracts and titles in family and friends names. As long as your property and wages are exempt, then the judgment is useless. The bad thing about doing something like this is a judgment will be abstracted against you for ten to twenty years or longer. This would hold you back from developing financially. There are no guarantees in life when depending on sources like family and friends. Uncontrollable circumstances like, death and divorce can occur.

When a creditor obtains a judgment against you, you become legally obligated to pay the creditor. You might have to fill out a form describing your income and property. If you put false information on the form, you will be committing perjury. You might have to appear in court to describe your income and property under oath. Perjury, making false statements, is a serious criminal offense. If you're earning an income or have non-exempt property, you will have to seek legal advice. If you have very little income and all your property is exempt, you probably cannot afford an attorney. If you cannot afford an attorney, then do not get one. Judges must follow the laws that govern them, but they're human beings too. If I had to pick from a judge, attorney, credit counselor or other interested party, I would pick a judge. No one else stands for fair play more than a judge. If you have to go to court and you have very little income and property, you better dress like it, feel like it and carry no cash with you, because the judgement creditor can ask for you to empty out your purse, pockets, and wallet. In some states, if you have valuable wedding rings, they can take them as partial payment for the judgement. If you are required to go to court over a judgement, you must stand up to your judgment in court, or you will become a criminal. *There is no reason in the world to become a criminal over debt.*

A *judgment creditor* is a creditor who has obtained a judgement against a debtor. Credit card creditors usually charge off the account instead of suing the debtor. You are still liable for charge-offs.

In ninety-five percent of the states, your wages can be garnished. To garnish your wages, they have to know where you work. To be judgment-proof in these states you would have to live on government assistance or have very little income and all your property would have to be exempt property.

Your creditor is informed of your employment by you whenever you fill out a loan application and it is reported to the credit bureaus. The creditor already knows where you work if you are employed with the same company you put on your original credit application. The creditor has a right to pull your credit file at any time. This will tell them where you're currently employed (if you filled out a credit application since you have moved or changed jobs). Your credit report will tell them other information such as your current address, phone number, relatives, and other information you wrote on your last credit application. They find you in other ways: by family members, friends, motor vehicle records, post office, banks, telephone companies and other sources obtainable by the public.

When a collection agency cannot find the original debtor, they will call several consumers with the same name as the original debtor and inform them of the original debt, hoping they trick the original debtor into admitting that it is his collection account. The collection agency might say that they are doing an asset investigation. All they are doing here is playing a guessing game and the game works. It does not mean they know who you are just because they have your Social Security number and name. You also have to worry about your former employer, family members or other sources giving information out about you. Collectors will try to fool them as well as you.

Bankruptcy Wait And See Technique

Creditors and bankruptcy attorneys do not like this technique which should be used only for debt that can be discharged. Thousands of unnecessary bankruptcies take place each month. These unnecessary bankruptcies represent dischargeable debt like credit card loans in the low to mid thousands. Often the creditor or collector threatens but takes no action, *scaring the consumer into filing an unnecessary bankruptcy.* Why do you think collection accounts or charge-offs exist? Because the creditor never sued the consumer who owed the debt.

Consumers with very little income can use this technique, but it can be tried by any consumer over-burdened with dischargeable debt. If you plan on using this technique, understand the bankruptcy laws and know what your exempt property is in your state. When using this technique you must take bankruptcy precautions and protect your exempt property. Everybody's personal financial situation is different; I will not be able to stipulate if you should or should not use this technique.

This technique can be referred to as *wait and file bankruptcy*. You can wait and see if the creditor will actually sue you. If and when you are served a summons to notify you that you have been sued, you could use the most lethal weapon and hated legal process in the credit and collection industry—bankruptcy.

Note: If you simply ask the credit card creditor in writing to charge-off your account, do not be surprised if the credit card creditor charges off your account. Their philosophy: you will pay off the account sometime in the future.

Bankruptcy will stop all lawsuits, judgments, wage garnishment and other legal remedies creditors and collectors use against consumers. Bankruptcy will stop a wage garnishment in all 50 states. The more dischargeable debts you have, the more beneficial bankruptcy will be. If you are going to file bankruptcy after the creditor files suit against you, you should inform the collector and creditor in writing. The creditor might think twice about suing you if it is a debt you can discharge in bankruptcy. Once the debt is erased in bankruptcy, the creditor will never receive any money for the debt. I would not try doing something like this unless I knew the debt would be dischargeable in bankruptcy. If you filed a Chapter 7 bankruptcy with in the last six years, this technique would be useless. The odds of the creditor suing you would definitely increase. Bankruptcy is a serious legal process, and will be covered further at the end of this presentation. If your creditor never sues you, your credit file will have a collection account or charge-off in it for seven years. Creditors, especially mortgage companies, do not like collection accounts or charge-offs.

You have the option of settling the account with the creditor or collector after your personal financial condition improves. In your letter to the creditor, tell them you plan on paying off the debt when your financial condition improves. You must make an effort to improve your financial condition. You will be making a start by giving up your credit cards.

Another thing bad about waiting to see if the creditor actually sues you is that you never know that the creditor sued you. Sometimes a consumer is surprised that a judgment has been entered against him because he never received notice that the creditor filed suit against him. He never knew that a lawsuit was filed against him because he never received the summons. The creditor was informed that the summons reached him. Actually the summons was thrown in the trash by the server and not served to the person being sued. *Trashing a summons* is illegal. You have a right to legal action if this happens to you. More important than taking legal action is to do what you originally planned on doing: file bankruptcy to stop the judgment.

When the server picks up the summons from the court, the server works for the court. It is a slim possibility that you will not receive your summons. The servers I know go out of the way to get the summons to the defendant.

If your account is already passed on to the collection department, you can do it all in one certified letter. In the same certified letter, you tell the collection agency your plans to file bankruptcy if you are sued; you can also use that same letter to stop the collector from communicating with you.

Bankruptcy
Chapter 7 or 13

We mentioned bankruptcy earlier, so let's examine it in detail here. Four types of bankruptcy can occur: Chapter 7, Chapter 11, Chapter 12, and Chapter 13. Corporations and a few individuals whose debts grew too large to qualify for a Chapter 13 use Chapter 11. Family farmers utilize Chapter 12. We will concentrate on Chapter 7 and Chapter 13 since these are the two bankruptcies that the average American consumer would use for debt relief.

Chapter 7 bankruptcy, known as *straight bankruptcy,* is the choice for the majority of consumers who have a large amount of unsecured debt. The consumer who files bankruptcy is known as a "debtor."

A Chapter 7 case from start to finish takes four to six months and usually requires *one* trip to the courthouse. You will sign your petition under oath. A bankruptcy petition asks the bankruptcy court for relief from your creditors. When filing the petition, the debtor will also have to file schedules describing the debtors' background, property and finances.

Filing the petition automatically stops the creditors from taking action against the debtor (on the day the petition is filed)—this means *no* communication between the creditor and debtor. The bankruptcy court appoints a *trustee* to oversee your case.

Filing the petition also prevents any creditor from continuing any *lawsuit, collection action, wage garnishment, foreclosure*, or any other action the creditor is using against the debtor. This move against your creditors is known as the *automatic stay,* which means that the creditors are stopped. The automatic stay is temporary. This gives the debtor time to work out secured loans like mortgages and automobile loans or to forfeit the secured property. The debtor will discharge all unsecured dischargeable debt and be liable only for priority debts and secured loans that were worked out with the creditor. The debtor will keep what his state classifies as exempt property and turn over non-exempt property to the trustee of the bankruptcy court. Few debtors lose any property in a Chapter 7.

If the debtor wants to keep any non-exempt property or has priority payments that need to be worked out, a Chapter 13 case would be the bankruptcy of choice. To file a Chapter 13, the debtor must have sound earnings. In a Chapter 13, the debtor would be able to keep all his property and still discharge some or all of the unsecured debt (credit card debt, medical bills and other dischargeable debts).

If non-exempt property is available, the trustee must sell the non-exempt property and pay the proceeds to the creditors.

As soon as possible after filing for bankruptcy, the creditors meeting is scheduled. The debtor is required to answer questions under oath about the property and finances. More than likely, the trustee will be the only one asking questions because creditors rarely attend the creditors meeting.

The trustee will file a final report with the court. A discharge of all dischargeable debts will be issued by the court. The debtors' Chapter 7 bankruptcy is complete. If the debtor fails to make the payments on secured loans after bankruptcy, the creditor can repossess or foreclose on the secured property as originally agreed. Bankruptcy does not eliminate secured debts like a mortgage or automobile loan, but it does allow you to give back the collateral and not be liable for the deficiency balance.

Chapter 13 Bankruptcy

Chapter 13 bankruptcy is a reorganization of debts or a payment plan. The debtor creates a budget similar to the one described in the chapter entitled "Get Tough With Plastic, Reorganize Your Debt Without Filing Bankruptcy," called *budget option*.

The debtor receives the same relief from creditors in a Chapter 13 payment plan as in a Chapter 7 straight bankruptcy. Chapter 13 bankruptcy is also known as the *wage earners plan* and is a voluntary repayment plan. A Chapter 13 must be approved by the court. Chapter 13 is usually used by consumers with sound earnings who are behind on their mortgage or automobile loans.

A Chapter 13 bankruptcy involves the same legal process as a Chapter 7 bankruptcy. The payment plan differs; it can be proposed for 36 months to a maximum time of 60 months. Part or all of your payment plan will include the value of your non-exempt property that you choose to keep. While you are in a Chapter 13 payment plan, you are under the supervision of a court-appointed trustee. The actual money paid to creditors depends on your income less expenses, the payment time frame, and exempt property. You make one monthly payment to the trustee who divides the payment up accordingly and distributes it to the creditors included in your payment plan. Debtors can include priority debts such as child support (which can be paid off over a period of time). The trustee is paid an administration fee deducted from the monthly payment.

If your current financial situation is distressed and you feel obligated to pay back all or a portion of your creditors, a Chapter 13 would be the bankruptcy of choice. This will give you the option of paying back your creditors 100% and it gives you time to reorganize your finances. In a Chapter 13 bankruptcy, the debtor can pay back anywhere from 1% to 100% of his unsecured "dischargeable" debts. In a Chapter 13 payment plan, creditors stop adding finance charges to unsecured debts like credit card loans. Priority debts and secured creditors are paid first.

The law requires bankruptcy of any type to be reported for a maximum of ten years. The banks have asked the credit bureaus to report a successfully completed Chapter 13 bankruptcy for seven years, hoping to lure the debtor into filing a Chapter 13 bankruptcy.

In a Chapter 7 bankruptcy, the banks receive nothing for their unsecured loans. In a Chapter 13 bankruptcy, the banks usually receive some payment for their unsecured loans. The disadvantage to a Chapter 13 bankruptcy is that your finances are in the hands of the court-appointed trustee during your payment plan time frame. In a Chapter 7 bankruptcy after your discharge, your finances are in your hands. After your Chapter 7 discharge, you could have your credit rating at A or B level in two years while with a Chapter 13 bankruptcy, you would still be under court supervision for credit approval. Being under court supervision for credit approval does not mean the court will not approve credit for the debtor.

The majority of the consumers claiming bankruptcy have very little property or income, one reason why Chapter 7 is the bankruptcy of choice. The debtor does not have a choice. The strategy for using Chapter 7 (if you have any non-exempt property) is to sell the non-exempt property and put the funds in exempt property, then file a Chapter 7 to discharge all dischargeable debts. Even if all your property is exempt property, you can still file a Chapter 13 bankruptcy.

Creditors and employers do not look at a successfully completed Chapter 13 as negative as a Chapter 7 because it is a *reorganization* compared to a Chapter 7 *liquidation*. Income earning consumers also file Chapter 13 because it is an excellent vehicle to help the consumer kick the debting habit. Every gainfully employed consumer contemplating bankruptcy should consider a Chapter 13. Some Chapter 13 bankruptcy trustees offer debt management classes and will report your successfully completed Chapter 13 plan to the credit bureaus.

No matter what type of bankruptcy you file, you should take advantage of your state exempt property and the laws that govern exempt property in your state. You can sell non-exempt property and put the money in exempt property before you file bankruptcy. You need to consult with the bankruptcy court or an experienced bankruptcy attorney in your state on exempt property transfers.

U. S. Code TITLE 11 Section 523, Exceptions to discharge.

Priority debts or non-dischargeable debts, debts that cannot be eliminated in bankruptcy.

1. State and federal taxes owed within the past two years before filing for bankruptcy, including money borrowed to pay those debts.
2. Alimony or child support.
3. Money, property, services, or credit obtained by fraud or misrepresentation.
4. Debts involving embezzlement, larceny, or fraud.
5. Fines and penalties payable to local, state, or federal government.
6. Student loans unless there is a showing of undue hardship on the debtor or dependents.
7. Debts owed as a result of willful and malicious injury to persons or property, operation of a motor vehicle while legally intoxicated.
8. Debts not listed in your bankruptcy petition.
9. Hot checks.
10. Property taxes.
11. Debts for fees and assessments for a condominium while occupying the unit.

Advice On 7 And 13

When you receive a credit application in the mail, notice that the creditor does *not* have a disclaimer on it warning that charging purchases could be risky and detrimental to the future of your personal finances.

Filing bankruptcy is giving up, telling your creditors, "Come and get it. I have had enough! (except you cannot have my wages and exempt property)."

I believe everybody deserves a second chance, but a third chance—that's pushing it. It is estimated that more than 15% of the individuals who file bankruptcy once do it again.

So how easy is it to obtain credit after bankruptcy? Open up your Yellow Pages and look up mortgage companies; call some of the mortgage companies and ask a mortgage loan officer, "How easy is it to obtain a mortgage after bankruptcy?"

You will be surprised. When you put an application in for a mortgage, the mortgage company usually requires you to have all delinquent or collection accounts brought current or paid off.

If you have a lot of delinquent or collection accounts in your credit file and you want to obtain a standard mortgage some time in the future, you might be better off discharging them in bankruptcy. You can obtain a standard mortgage within two years with the same interest rate as a good credit applicant if you make an effort to reestablish new credit.

The same applies to an auto loan if you work your way back up to "A" type credit. You can have "A" type credit *within two years*!

Refer to "A" type credit or good credit, "Credit Ratings" on page 27.

In a few months after your bankruptcy petition is registered through the court, you should start receiving creditors promotional applications for secured credit cards. If you want to re-establish credit using a secured credit card, you can keep your name on the credit bureaus' promotional mailing lists. Secured credit cards are one of the easiest and most common ways to reestablish credit.

Remember that other ways do exist to re-establish credit besides using a secured credit card. After four years, most businesses start overlooking bankruptcy. If you're still paying your secured creditors and utilities on time after your bankruptcy is discharged, you are already ahead of the game because some creditors will look at this positively. Other creditors will require you to establish new credit. Keep good records of your mortgage or rent payments. Credit bureaus do not keep a consumers' payment history to landlords. A large credit line on an unsecured credit card will be the hardest credit to obtain after bankruptcy. If credit card debt is one of the reasons you filed bankruptcy in the first place, who needs it anyway?

You do not have to establish new credit in order to buy a house. You have other options to obtain a mortgage. You can use one of the techniques I explained to you in "Mortgage Money & A Home For Everybody" on page 25. I have learned that programs like Shoppers Anonymous, Debtors Anonymous, Gamblers Anonymous and other 12-step support programs believe you should pay back 100% of your debt. I am non-biased on this concept. I said earlier, "You have to take care of yourself as long it is within the limits of the law."

Our Congress enacted the bankruptcy laws for you to use (but not abuse) them. Everybody deserves a second chance. If you claim bankruptcy a third or fourth time, that's no ones' business but yours. The law allows you to claim Chapter 7 bankruptcy six years after your last discharge and a Chapter 13 even sooner. Just because you do not pay back your creditors 100% of what you owe them does not mean you won't be able to join a 12-step support group—they will accept anyone. I think it is a good idea for everybody to at least visit one of the anonymous support groups even if they do not have a problem or habit.

The final decision will be entirely up to you to decide: who and how to pay back your creditors.

Consumer Credit Counseling Service and other debt management organizations advertise that bankruptcy is a ten-year mistake. Joining a debt management organization like Consumer Credit Counseling Services could be a worse mistake than bankruptcy. In the two following examples, several consumers lost thousands of dollars that they could have otherwise kept if they had claimed bankruptcy sooner.

If you're in a debt management organization and you're taking money out of what your state includes as exempt property in order to meet your financial obligations, you would be able to keep this property in bankruptcy.

In the second example, the debtor is paying for debts that are dischargeable in bankruptcy. Debt management organizations should be called "credit card management organizations." *All 100% of your credit card debt can be discharged in bankruptcy.* Now you know why they advertise against bankruptcy: they need the credit card business to stay in business.

If you are that far over-extended, you probably would not be able to obtain credit for several years, and that is only if you brought your debt-to-income ratio down. Filing bankruptcy could be to your benefit in obtaining credit even sooner. Having a large debt load can look just as bad (or worse) to a creditor or employer than a bankruptcy in your credit file.

All creditors look at your credit file before issuing you credit and some employers look at credit files before hiring. You can always pick up the telephone and call some employers and ask them if they require a credit file on prospective employees. Bankruptcy laws prohibit employers from discriminating against debtors for filing bankruptcy. You will not lose your job for filing bankruptcy. The chance of your current employer knowing you claimed bankruptcy is very slim unless you tell someone. In some cases, bankruptcy courts require wage withholding to fund your Chapter 13 payment plan (then your employer *will* know about your bankruptcy).

To get around this, ask the bankruptcy court to automatically draft your personal checking account to fund the Chapter 13 payment plan. Tell the bankruptcy court that even though it is illegal to discriminate against bankrupt consumers, it could jeopardize your job. Your past work history and performance will account for your opportunity to advance more than a credit report.

The new law requires all employers (just like creditors) to get your permission before obtaining a copy of your credit report. If you're worried about a creditor or employer asking about your bankruptcy, learn how to answer their questions. They do not want to hear excuses like overspending, or things that you had no control over, even though in some cases you may have had no control over your divorce. Some creditors frown at divorce as an excuse.

Creditors and employers like to hear things you had no control over such as unemployment, a cut in salary or medical bills. If you tell them "medical bills" caused your bankruptcy but all you have in your credit file are discharged credit card debts, they might be a little suspicious (even if you tell them that you charged all your medical bills). Some people without health insurance have charged all their medical bills to obtain medical help.

Employers that I am familiar with do not give out salary histories. You can always call your former employer and ask them what type of information they surrender to other employers. Employers usually require a credit check on positions that handle money or expensive equipment. I know several hard working and honest consumers who have positions of this type but even they claimed bankruptcy. Chapter 13 reorganization always looks better than Chapter 7 liquidation.

Some mortgage companies, employers and creditors are more understanding than others, particularly if your debting situation took years to unfold. An example of such a slowly unfolding scenario would be mounting credit card debt discharged in bankruptcy; you maintain a commitment to not acquiring balances on your credit cards. If you obtained or retained a credit card in bankruptcy, you should pay off the balance monthly. Your credit file needs to support your commitment to acquiring no further debt. If your goal is to acquire a collateralized loan like a mortgage or automobile, you can accomplish it at competitive interest rates.

George consulted with me twenty-four months into his Chapter 13 payment plan. He was a client of National Credit Counseling Services for 12 months before he filed bankruptcy. Six months after he joined National Credit Counseling Services, he borrowed twenty thousand dollars out of his individual retirement account in order to meet his financial obligations for his family.

George was paying thirteen hundred dollars a month in dischargeable debt. The majority of that thirteen hundred dollars a month was going to National Credit Counseling Services.

George could not handle being strapped for money every month. His family was making enough sacrifices. George was worried about his family and his employer knowing about his bankruptcy filing. He started investigating bankruptcy. George found an experienced bankruptcy attorney. He decided to file a Chapter 13 payment plan. All of the property George owned was exempt property except for the rental property he had just put on the market. George paid all his secured creditors on time—including his mortgage, car note and individual retirement loan. He stopped paying his unsecured creditors the thirteen hundred dollars a month two months before he filed. Since George continued to pay his secured creditors as agreed, they were not included in his Chapter 13 monthly payment plan. Only George's dischargeable debts—which were the thirteen hundred dollars a month—were included in his Chapter 13 monthly payment plan.

He received a few phone calls but mostly letters from creditors until they received the news from the court about him filing bankruptcy. George's Chapter 13 payment plan required him to pay two hundred dollars a month for 60 months because of the equity he had in his rental property and his excess income—two hundred dollars a month compared to thirteen hundred dollars a month! That is an *eleven hundred dollar a month difference.* George was going eleven hundred dollars a month over budget. George had eleven hundred dollars a month more to support his family.

George said he never saw anybody but his attorney, the trustee and other consumers who were filing bankruptcy. No creditors showed up for his *creditors meeting* (sometimes referred to as the *341 meeting*). Creditors rarely show up for this meeting. George did not want to tell his wife until he was well into his Chapter 13 payment plan. After he told her, she still has a hard time believing it, because she never saw or heard from anybody. Neither his employer nor any of his coworkers know that he filed bankruptcy.

Two years after George filed bankruptcy, his biggest regret was he wished he had filed bankruptcy sooner and was more prepared. The twenty thousand dollar individual retirement account was exempt property (not to mention the thirteen hundred dollars a month to National Credit Counseling Services for his creditors). He said he would have sold the rental house before he filed bankruptcy and put the money in exempt property, then filed a Chapter 7. I might have asked him to consider a Chapter 13—even if all his property were exempt property.

When he told me he had sold the rental property, I asked him if I could look at his petition. After I reviewed his petition and asked him a few questions, I told him to call his attorney and to tell him he should be in a thirty-six months payment plan, not a sixty-month plan. Additionally, I found that his excess income had changed and he was paying too much into the plan. George said when he called his attorney, the attorney tried to talk him into converting to a Chapter 7 bankruptcy until he threw the rest of the questions at his attorney.

Converting a Chapter 13 to a Chapter 7 would have cost George a lot more money and it would have added five more years (for a total of ten years) for the bankruptcy to appear in his credit file. A Chapter 7 filing would have made the attorney a lot more money than modifying a Chapter 13 plan. George's modified Chapter 13 payment plan required him to pay *fifty dollars* a month for 11 more months. After that he will have successfully completed a Chapter 13 plan. Even though George paid back only a small percentage of his dischargeable debts, he still successfully completed a Chapter 13 bankruptcy. If any changes in your original petition favor that you be informed of them, then consult with an attorney.

Note: In a Chapter 13, if your attorney puts you in a 60 month plan instead of a 36 month plan, make sure you know exactly why. Remember, your finances are under court supervision in a Chapter 13 payment plan. The court supervision law might change in order to benefit the debtor. Even when dealing only with dischargeable debt (in some circumstances), being in a 36-month Chapter 13 can be more beneficial to a debtor than a Chapter 7 liquidation.

Joining a debt management program may be the thing to do before you file bankruptcy. This will keep the creditors off your back and give you a chance to prepare for your bankruptcy filing. In this case you would want to negotiate the lowest monthly payment possible with the debt management organization. This will tarnish your credit file. These are the same creditors that will be included in your bankruptcy and it will keep the creditors at bay until you call them with the news. The strategy here is to make your bankruptcy filing as easy as possible. Your creditors will hold off longer if you are a member of a debt management organization before they start calling you.

One consumer told me that he filed bankruptcy the easy way. He continued to make his priority and secured payments on time. He filed bankruptcy after his credit card payments became thirty days late. The same day he filed bankruptcy, he called all his credit card creditors (whose debts he was discharging in his petition) and informed them of his bankruptcy filing. Not one creditor called him. All he lost was thirty days of the ninety-day property transfer to the trustee. He preferred to make one more month's payment to his creditors than to worry about the creditors calling him at work. If you file bankruptcy, you can notify most major banks over the phone and they will note in your account your bankruptcy filing. You shouldn't receive any phone calls from creditors, and they do not have to call you.

If the creditors do call you, tell them you're filing bankruptcy. Most creditors will not call you back as long as they hear from the clerk of the court about your bankruptcy filing. For a while, you will still receive computer-generated letters and statements in the mail.

Any debts paid to creditors 90 days before bankruptcy filing are surrendered to the trustee. Most bankruptcy filings are made ninety days after payment to the last creditor to be discharged in bankruptcy. Actually this means only that the credit card payment is 60-days late. Remember the 30 day grace period.

Chapter 13 bankruptcy is often used by consumers with a regular income but who are behind on their mortgage payment or car note and threatened by creditors with foreclosure or repossession. If a consumer has no unsecured dischargeable debt—and has tried to the best of his ability to work with creditors on his mortgage or car note to stop foreclosure or repossession—then filing Chapter 13 bankruptcy is the last resort and most powerful weapon.

A debtor can work out payment arrangements for mortgages, auto loans and priority debts while under court supervision in a Chapter 13. Since priority debts are not dischargeable in bankruptcy, you can include priority debts in your Chapter 13 payment plan. For example, if you owe federal back taxes (which are priority debt), you might be able to include your IRS debt in your Chapter 13 payment plan. This can stop the tax bill from accumulating interest. One of the most common priority debts included in a Chapter 13 payment plan is *child support*.

If a consumer is struggling with a large amount of dischargeable debt and falling behind on the mortgage or car note, the consumer should do something about the dischargeable debt and bring the mortgage or car note current. Several options exist for dealing with dischargeable debt.

If you decide to file bankruptcy by using one of the do-it-yourself *bankruptcy kits*, make absolutely sure that all of your property is *exempt property* in your state. Seek the input of an experienced bankruptcy attorney in your state. A lot of consumers file their own bankruptcy because they are unemployed and their money is tight. They spend a lot of their free time studying bankruptcy at the law library. I personally feel they would be better off looking for a job with that free time. One way to file your own bankruptcy is to seek legal advice from an attorney, and then have a paralegal do the required typing to complete the petition. You do not have to tell the attorney you are seeking legal advice for filing your own bankruptcy. You can find paralegals in your Yellow Pages or on the Internet. Some of these paralegals specialize in preparing bankruptcy petitions.

Read the section on "Exempt Property" in the back of the book, how debtors who filed their own bankruptcy made a major mistake.

You can find a good lawyer that specializes in bankruptcy by using your Yellow Pages and by calling the Bar Association for your community. Places such as an Employees Assistance Program can offer other references. You do not need to pay big bucks for a bankruptcy attorney. The high-volume experienced bankruptcy attorney is fine—he handles more cases and costs less. Do not get the cheapest, highest volume bankruptcy attorney that advertises in your local free paper. If you are considering a Chapter 13 bankruptcy, make sure you find an attorney with Chapter 13 experience.

Too many consumers wait until the last minute before filing bankruptcy, then end up with an attorney that does not give their case adequate attention. Prepare a list of questions before you go to your first visit with an attorney. Take a pen, note pad, last month's pay stubs and a list of your debts, along with your list of questions on your first visit. If you sense that this attorney will not adequately represent you, then go to the next attorney that you researched. After your first visit to an attorney, go home and look over your case. Ask yourself, "Is it appropriate to obtain another attorney's opinion?" If you follow these guidelines, your attorney will give your case more attention.

Even though bankruptcy will cost you five hundred to two thousand dollars, in the long run an experienced bankruptcy attorney will save you money. For example, an experienced Chapter 13 bankruptcy attorney will help you on your budget. In Chapter 7 and 13 bankruptcies he knows how to value your property in order for you to receive the most out of your exempt property. Many consumers that filed bankruptcy were surprised how low their attorney appraised their exempt property. Your exempt property is usually valued at garage sale prices and the courts do not like having garage sales. Do yourself a favor and know what your state property exemptions are, even if you do not file bankruptcy.

You do not want to get stuck in a Chapter 13 bankruptcy if you think a Chapter 7 is more appropriate for your personal situation. It's your decision. Attorneys make more money off Chapter 13 filings. If you convert your Chapter 13 to a Chapter 7, you will be paying for *two* bankruptcies.

Down the road you can modify your Chapter 13 bankruptcy payment plan if your income or expenses change. I strongly encourage you to finish a Chapter 13 bankruptcy if you start in a Chapter 13. What state you live in can be a factor in deciding which type of bankruptcy to file, Chapter 7 or Chapter 13. The specifics of exempt property vary greatly from state to state. For the same reason, the laws of your state can be a factor in deciding whether to file bankruptcy at all.

A good bankruptcy attorney will not charge you for your initial consultation, nor will he pressure you into filing. In a Chapter 13 bankruptcy, your attorney can be paid out over your scheduled payment plan. Your initial fee in a Chapter 13 bankruptcy should cost you approximately 20%, and the rest can be paid out over time. If your Chapter 13 bankruptcy costs one thousand dollars you would have to pay only two hundred dollars down. Some attorneys offer payment plans for Chapter 7 bankruptcy, too.

Do not forget (ever) that you hired this attorney for his services. If you do not file bankruptcy, he will not make any money. He wants your money and you want good service. Before you file bankruptcy, find out what the maximum cost will be for his services in writing. He is required to put the total cost for his services in your petition. The more informed you are about bankruptcy, the more attention your attorney will give your case.

Honesty about your personal finances with your attorney is vital in bankruptcy.

You cannot discharge a debt to a creditor of one thousand dollars or more that you used to purchase luxury goods, services and cash advances within the last 60 days in a Chapter 7 bankruptcy. You can still file bankruptcy but if you think you are guilty of the 60-day limit, this is another reason to consult with an experienced bankruptcy attorney in your state. You can include purchases of luxury goods, services and cash advances to a creditor of one thousand dollars or more in a Chapter 13 bankruptcy. The reason for the 60-day limit on one thousand dollars or more is easy to understand. A consumer should not be allowed to discharge debts he ran up on a last minute vacation to Las Vegas days before the consumer files bankruptcy.

Before filing bankruptcy, take the cash from the sale of nonexempt property and put the cash into exempt property. This is legal. For example, John lived in Texas with a large amount of dischargeable debt. John knew his financial condition was deteriorating. He did not want to end up like so many other consumers who wait until the last minute to file bankruptcy. These people would have to sell off a lot of their exempt property to meet their monthly expenses. John owned a boat and motorcycle, which are non-exempt property. He ran ads in his local newspaper for several weeks trying to sell the boat and motorcycle. He retained the advertisements; he put in the newspaper (as evidence) that he was selling his property at what the market would bring in a reasonable amount of time. When he sold the boat and motorcycle, he took the cash and used it to pay off a second mortgage he had on his home, which is exempt property. Texas has a generous homestead exemption. John filed a Chapter 7 bankruptcy after paying off his second mortgage. His attorney asked him how he knew about property transfers. What John did was completely legal.

John retained a larger net worth after his bankruptcy discharge by transferring the cash from non-exempt property and putting it in exempt property. John received other benefits from these property transfers as well. He did not have to surrender the property to creditors or worry about his attorney putting him in a Chapter 13 to retain the non-exempt property. You need to make these property transfers as far in advance of your bankruptcy filing as possible. If you are thinking about filing bankruptcy, you need to consult with the bankruptcy court or an experienced bankruptcy attorney in your state before making these non-exempt property transfers. Bankruptcy courts in some states are more lenient than courts in other states on property transfers. Even if you do not file bankruptcy, you should protect your exempt property (especially if you have a large dischargeable debt load). Do not do anything stupid before filing for bankruptcy. Stupid actions would be giving your house to your brother. This is a fraud. You can go to jail for committing fraud. You will not go to jail for not paying your debts.

Now, if you sold your house to your brother at fair market value and turn around and rented it from him, that is legal. The Bankruptcy Code was established by our Congress to help out the honest consumer in debt over his head because of poor spending habits or misfortune, and give this consumer a fresh start. If you gave your house to your brother and it was already exempt property in your state, then it would not matter at all because your creditors had no right to the property in the first place.

Exempt property varies greatly from state to state. In some states, someone can still have a net worth of one million dollars after their bankruptcy is discharged; in other states, the same individual could be left with the basic essentials after their bankruptcy is discharged. If I had to file bankruptcy, I would definitely relocate to the state where I could put my money in an exempt homestead or protect my individual retirement account and keep my million-dollar net worth. I could move back after my bankruptcy is discharged. Federal law requires you to have a residence in the state in which you file bankruptcy for one hundred and eighty days before your file bankruptcy.

Do not feel bad about not paying back creditors for unsecured loans. The banks make a fortune off their high interest credit card business. Your loss is factored into the high interest rates you and all their other customers are charged. Think how long you've been paying high interest rates on your credit cards or other unsecured loans. The creditor will write the loan off as a loss. A consumer who had filed bankruptcy told me, "I feel bad about the other credit card customers who pay for my loss."

I said, "There is no reason to feel bad. You have been paying high interest rates for years for other consumers who filed bankruptcy . You're also in the same situation as the credit card customers you feel sorry for. You're paying taxes for all types of losses, including loans. Your tax dollars pay for defaulted loans that the government guarantees."

If you are married, the spouse with the most dischargeable debts usually claims bankruptcy and discharges the majority of the unsecured debt. Jointly owned property and debts will not be affected if paid for as agreed. This will leave the other spouse able to provide credit for the family.

In some cases, married couples might not have a choice; they might have to file bankruptcy jointly if all or most of the couple's accounts are joint or if the couple needs to double up on their state exemptions.

The majority of consumers who claimed bankruptcy forfeited all of their credit cards because of high balances on all of them. They then obtained a debit card or secured credit card. If you have one without a balance, then you do not have to claim it in your Chapter 7 petition. In a Chapter 13 payment plan, you need to take up the credit card issue with the bankruptcy court. The key word in a Chapter 13 payment plan is *court approval for credit*. This does not include secured credit cards or debit cards. You can obtain a secured credit card, authorized credit card or debit card. Read Chapter Four if you need more information on this subject.

While some states offer generous exemptions for vehicles, other states offer none. If in your state you are not allowed enough of an exemption to obtain a vehicle suited for your needs, you still have several options. You can sell your current vehicle, then put the money in exempt property. When you purchase another vehicle, borrow enough against it in order to meet your state exemption or borrow against your current vehicle and put the funds in exempt property. You can borrow from a close friend or family member. Consult with an experienced bankruptcy attorney in your state on this issue. Read Chapter Four.

A friend consulted with me about his credit union. He was worried that they would find out about his filing bankruptcy if he decided to. I asked him if he had any loans at his credit union. He had one automobile loan that he would have to list in his petition if he filed bankruptcy. I told him to sell that vehicle and pay off the balance at his credit union. Then go purchase another vehicle for the minimum down payment and obtain the financing through the dealership. Remember, an automobile loan is the easiest loan to acquire. He still had a decent credit file so he was able to obtain a decent interest rate. When he filed bankruptcy, he agreed to pay for the new vehicle as originally agreed in his contact with the dealer. This consumer benefitted in two ways. 1) He acquired a new vehicle that would carry him a few years while he had the bankruptcy statement in his credit file. This would give him time to reestablish credit if desired. 2) He did not have to list his credit union in his petition as a creditor. Even though he did not plan on giving back his automobile to the credit union, he would still have to list the credit union as a creditor in his petition. The credit union would not have touched his checking or savings account because he was going to continue to pay for the collateral as agreed. He did not want his credit union knowing for personal and employment reasons. If he filed a Chapter 13 bankruptcy, he would be able to include the new car payment in his budget. You must list all your creditors in your petition.

Any lending institution in which you have a checking or savings account and owe a debt that you plan on discharging in bankruptcy can withdraw funds from your checking or savings account to cover the debt you owe the lending institution. They do not have to wait for you to file bankruptcy; they can withdraw the funds as soon as they find out. They find out when the consumer opens his mouth. Be careful about discussing your personal finances with anyone. You do not need to close the accounts—just withdraw all your money from all checking and savings accounts at any lending institutions whose debt you plan to discharge. Remember, this does not include exempt property like an individual retirement account if it is exempt in your state. If it is a collateralized loan (like an automobile loan that you will continue to pay for as originally agreed), you do not have to worry about emptying out your accounts. Empty out accounts only at lending institutions where you plan on discharging debts. The key word is discharging.

After your bankruptcy case is filed, the creditor receives a copy of your petition and schedules. Some creditors might compare your schedules to the last loan application you completed. If the creditor finds any major deviations on the loan application compared to the schedules, an action to have the loan declared non-dischargeable can be filed by the creditor. This is rare, but more common in a Chapter 7 bankruptcy, because the creditor does not receive any compensation for dischargeable debts. The more recent your loan application, the more likely a creditor will examine your schedules.

If you file bankruptcy and you are due a tax refund, the bankruptcy trustee can take the refund. I am familiar with cases where the consumer's tax refund was not even an issue. With a large tax refund, it can be an issue. Try to collect your tax refund before you file bankruptcy. The state you live in will be a factor when deciding what to do with tax refunds.

If you do not have health insurance, consider purchasing some type of health insurance policy, even one with a large deductible and a small premium. You could find yourself in the same situation as before you filed bankruptcy.

You can file a Chapter 7 bankruptcy every six years from the date you filed your last Chapter 7. If you originally filed a Chapter 13 bankruptcy, you can still file a Chapter 7 bankruptcy without any time limitations. This is one of the advantages of filing a Chapter 13 bankruptcy. Even with these bankruptcy reliefs, if a health emergency arises, you will not get the medical attention an insured patient will receive. If you file a Chapter 13, you should definitely purchase health insurance before you fill out the forms describing your budget so health insurance will be included in your expenses.

More and more bankruptcy judges are finding reasons for gainfully employed consumers to file a Chapter 13 bankruptcy even if their original plans were to file Chapter 7. When you do your first budget, increase your legitimate expenses before you turn your budget over to your attorney. For example, increase your retirement withholding's or activities for your children. These are legitimate expenses that will reduce your monthly payment into the Chapter 13 plan. Make sure your retirement withholding's and your retirement plan are exempt property in your state.

If your annual salary is thirty thousand dollars a year and you have six thousand dollars of unsecured dischargeable debt, it would be ridiculous for you to file bankruptcy. You're better off trying to negotiate with your creditors, joining a debt management organization, or selling off property to reduce your debt load. If your unsecured dischargeable debts are more than 60 percent of your annual salary, you are a candidate for bankruptcy. For example, if annual salary is fifty thousand dollars and your total dischargeable debt is thirty thousand dollars, you should have already taken bankruptcy precautions unless you have already filed bankruptcy.

These are examples—everybody's financial situation is different. No two bankruptcies are alike. Some consumers filing bankruptcy have very little dischargeable debt.

For many consumers, the majority of their net worth resides in their IRA, 401k or other retirement plan. Your retirement plan is usually exempt property. Most consumers' retirement plans are protected by the federal law known as Employee Retirement Income Security Act or ERISA. Even if your state exemptions do not list an ERISA-covered plan as exempt property, it can still be exempt property. ERISA or not, your retirement plan is another issue you need to take up with an experienced bankruptcy attorney in your state.

What if your retirement plan is not exempt and you are overburdened with debt? You might have a relative or friend that lives in a state next door where your retirement plan is exempt property. Establish a residence in the state next door, then file bankruptcy in that state. For renters, this is relatively easy. How much equity do you have in your home? To a creditor, your home might be worthless, even though it is not worthless to you.

Does your state require you to own your home for a certain amount of time or file your homestead through the public records office before you can claim the homestead exemption? If your state did not allow a homestead exemption and you filed bankruptcy, the bankruptcy trustee is not going to take your home from you if you owe more on your home than it is worth. This includes your mortgage, any other equity loans, liens and taxes you owe against your home. Refer to the end of Chapter Two. What is your home worth?

If you file bankruptcy and have a deficiency balance or negative equity in your home or car, you can give the collateral back to the creditor and you will not be liable for the deficiency balance.

How much equity do you have in your home? How much of your equity is exempt from creditors? Is your retirement plan exempt? What about your income tax refund, automobile and all other exemptions? This is when you get the pen and paper out. You need to call the bankruptcy court or attorney and ask about your state exemptions. State exempt property laws do not stop the Internal Revenue Service from seizing property.

Before a major corporation files bankruptcy, the board of directors sits behind closed doors and devotes a lot of time preparing for their bankruptcy filing. The same applies to wealthy individuals who file bankruptcy and end up with a million dollars net worth. You as a consuming American have the same rights to prepare yourself before you file for bankruptcy. I have seen too many consumers file too late or too soon, most of them unprepared. The most critical factor when filing for bankruptcy is preparation.

There are no limits on your future ability to acquire property or wealth after your bankruptcy is discharged. Several self-made millionaires claimed some type of bankruptcy before acquiring their wealth. Some of these millionaires are well-known. Restrictions may apply if you acquired an inheritance, life insurance or settlements within the six months after bankruptcy these funds may be available for creditors.

Attorneys (just like everybody else) can make mistakes. You must review your schedules in your petition and make sure everything is correct.

You should know if your financial condition is deteriorating. Do not wait until you've drained your exempt property or until your stressed out from creditors or collectors calling. Be gentle on yourself! Take control of the situation and act accordingly. Filing bankruptcy can be a strong character development for certain individuals.

It is almost impossible for anyone you know personally to know you filed bankruptcy unless you tell them. One gentleman's wife does not even know her husband filed for bankruptcy three years ago. I personally feel it is her business but his business is his business and not mine. I will not disclose his business to anyone.

Do not let an attorney persuade you into making a decision that is not beneficial to you. Some attorneys love to convert a Chapter 13 into a Chapter 7. That is paying for two bankruptcies. Make sure your original Chapter 13 budget accounts for all of your expenses. You are better off over-estimating your expenses than underestimating them. The majority of consumers underestimate their original budget. If you modify your original budget, the judge or trustee in your state might not approve it. You cannot over-estimate expenses like mortgage payments, taxes, car notes and the like. These payments are fixed payments. You would be committing perjury by over-estimating fixed payments. Clothing, car maintenance and so forth are not fixed payments. Do not underestimate these types of expenses in your budget. If you ever developed a budget before, you know what I am talking about.

It might be a good idea to start a budget now.

Even though Chapter 7 is by far the bankruptcy of choice, two bills floating around in Congress might change that. These bills require debtors to file a Chapter 13. This is one reason why I covered Chapter 13 like I did.

Always be nice. You get more with sweetness than bitterness. If you're in a situation where you feel bothered, avoid that situation. For example, if you feel uncomfortable with your attorney, you can obtain legal services elsewhere.

When your attorney starts asking you questions, answer back with informative answers; do not just say yes and no. You want your attorney to give your case the attention it deserves.

Credit:
Marriage And Divorce
Things You Should Know

A few pointers on marriage and divorce (relating to credit) can save you a lot of money to spend on other things in the future.

If you are planning for divorce, obtain copies of your credit reports beforehand. After the divorce, get another credit report.

If you're married, you are entitled to share credit information. Let's say that one of you has a bad credit file; the other one has a good credit file. Write to the credit bureaus and ask them to *merge* your credit files. Both credit files will have the same information after the credit bureaus merge the two files. After they're merged, the one with the original good credit file writes back to the credit bureaus, asking the credit bureaus to remove the negative information that was merged with the positive information. The credit bureaus will remove the negative information. The result: you will have one credit file with both positive and negative information. The other credit file will have positive information only. As long as you are married, this technique is legal. This technique is used by credit repair clinics for individuals who are not married.

You should establish credit in your name exclusively. If you are married and your husband runs into financial trouble, loses his job, claims bankruptcy, divorce, separation or death, you with your own credit file will be able to provide credit for yourself and your family. Even in community property states you can establish individual credit. You are both liable for consigned or joint accounts, so you should keep these to a minimum. If you are married, utility bills represent the exception to the joint account rule. Utility accounts should be joint accounts if something happens. You do not have to worry about making a deposit to the utility company.

If you are a married woman and apply for individual credit, the creditor cannot require you to use your husband as a co-signer. In other words the creditor cannot discriminate against a married woman. If you are denied credit on an individual basis, the creditor must give you the reason why in writing.

Your ex-spouse can damage your credit history and cause you to be liable for debts you did not charge. If you are considering separation, divorce, or if your relationship is on the rocks, you should close all joint accounts. If you cannot transfer the balance to an individual account or afford to pay off the balance, you can send a letter by certified mail giving back the credit card to the creditor and stop all credit privileges on the joint account. Continue to make regular payments to the creditor. In most circumstances, giving back the credit card is probably the thing to do. In some community property states, you are liable for individual accounts as well as joint accounts.

This is a good time to try negotiating a lower interest rate on your current balance. If your spouse does not agree to giving back the credit card to the creditor, you can say you are giving it back in order to negotiate a lower interest rate. Even if your spouse disagrees, communicate what you are doing before you do it. A divorce decree does not cancel your obligation to pay back joint accounts incurred during marriage. Look in back of the book in Public Documents for "Credit and Divorce."

If you are soon to be divorced, you should protect your credit and credit report by removing your name from the credit bureaus promotional mailing list and other junk mail solicitations. Make sure all your mail is being forwarded to your new address. Destroy all credit applications you receive at your current address. I am not saying your ex-spouse is a thief, but some ex-spouses are. Ex-spouses have filled out pre-approved credit applications by forging the other's signature, used the credit cards and ruined the ex-spouse's good credit.

Credit card companies do not verify signatures. They are just thrilled that someone got suckered into their pre-approved credit card application. But when it comes time to prove to the creditor that your signature has been forged, that is another story.

If you are the individual who retains a mortgage or home equity loan after a divorce, the mortgage company is not required to remove the other ex-spouse's name from the jointly-held mortgage. Since it is a collateralized loan and you are the one retaining the property, removing the other's name is not that big of a deal (if you protect your interest in the property using the required legal instrument).

Two of these instruments are a quitclaim deed and a special warranty deed. The spouse conveying or transferring the property legally deeds the interests over to the spouse retaining the property. This protects the interest of the one retaining the property, even if the name of the one who transferred the property is not removed from the mortgage. After recording the legal instrument through the public records office, you must send a copy to the mortgage company. The mortgage company might remove the name of the one who transferred the property from the account even though the mortgage company is not required to. If the spouse transferring the property is not removed from the mortgage, the spouse transferring the property over should not have anything to worry about, especially if the home is worth more than what is owed on it. If your mortgage company reports to the credit bureaus, then both spouses will continue to see their names credited for the mortgage to each of their credit files. Since this is considered a joint account to the mortgage company, both spouses are still responsible for payment.

When applying for a loan, the spouse who transferred the property over will show the creditor the legal instrument or divorce decree showing transfer of ownership, and the mortgage will not be included as an expense on their loan application. Refinancing as an individual or after remarriage is always a possibility.

In the example below, exempt property can be a loan you took out against your retirement account or a home equity loan in order to pay your spouse the share of the divorce settlement. A loan against your retirement account is a priority payment and must be paid under any circumstances. If you are going to get a divorce and you have a large dischargeable debt load that you and your spouse acquired during marriage, it might be to your advantage to acquire more exempt property in exchange for more dischargeable debt that you can discharge in bankruptcy.

I am familiar with a case where one spouse was forced into bankruptcy after the divorce due to loss of her ex-husband's income. If she had acquired more dischargeable debt from him in exchange for exempt property (like not having to borrow against her retirement account in order to pay him off), she would have been able to discharge more of the debt in bankruptcy. This would have left her with more exempt property and no priority payment to pay off, as in the loan against her retirement account.

In some circumstances, doing something like this could force your ex-spouse into bankruptcy because the creditors can come after the other spouse for payment if the other spouse is still obligated by law to pay. If you are contemplating something of this nature, you should consult with an experienced bankruptcy attorney in your state.

Exempt Property

Dealing with exempt property[1] using information from inexpensive sources like books and the Internet rather than counseling with an attorney can be costly. For example, numerous consumers filed their own bankruptcies—thinking their retirement plan was exempt property. After their bankruptcy petitions were filed through the courts, the same consumers found out that their retirement plans were not exempt property to the bankruptcy court in their state. That means their retirement plans were not exempt property, therefore the money was available to creditors listed in their bankruptcy petition.

What could these consumers have done to save their retirement plans? Instead of filing bankruptcy, they could have tried negotiating a payment plan with their creditors or established a residency in a nearby state before filing bankruptcy. Consumers do not know how to value their auto, home and other types of exempt property. These are just a few examples of many. I strongly encourage you to visit with an experienced bankruptcy attorney in your state on exempt property issues. Usually the attorney will not even charge you for this service. You might be able to correspond with the attorney or attorneys through the mail. You might want to correspond with an attorney out of state.

Florida, Texas, Kansas and Iowa offer unlimited homestead exemptions. Florida is a debtors' haven. Remember the former corporate raider P.B. who bought a $6 million house in Tampa then filed Chapter 7 bankruptcy for protection from creditors? P.B. later paid back some of his debts that he did not have to. The stories go on and on about debtors filing bankruptcy in Florida and walking away with a million-dollar net worth after their debts

---

1. I chose not to list your state exempt property in this edition. It is relatively easy to get a list of your current state exempt property. You can find your state exempt property easily if you have access to the Internet. The bookstores offer books and bankruptcy kits that list your state exemptions.

are discharged in bankruptcy. I don't think any of them paid back their creditors like P.B. did.

I like the story about the mortgage broker who went bankrupt in Virginia. The homestead exception in Virginia is only $5,000 dollars. You are allowed to keep other exempt property, including "one horse." The mortgage broker bought one horse—one *race* horse—worth $800,000, just weeks before filing bankruptcy. After his bankruptcy was discharged, he was allowed to keep his one horse. One of my friends said, "If he was one of the creditors included in the mortgage brokers bankruptcy, he would have put his Smith and Wesson to work on the horse."

Consumers complain and fuss about debtors protecting their net worth from creditors. In the past, I did not think it was fair either. There is more to it: *asset allocation*. If it were not for unlimited homestead exemptions in some states, the debtor would take his money out of America and find protection elsewhere. This protection goes beyond Swiss bank accounts. Swiss banks would be last on my list if I had to seek protection from creditors. I do not have to worry about it because I do not plan on being rich. Texas, where I live, offers unlimited homestead protection along with other generous exemptions, including 120 chicks. If I have to seek protection, I would start a chick farm.

Even though your wages cannot be garnished in Texas, Florida and Pennsylvania, bankruptcy laws protect debtors from wage garnishments in all states. This does not mean you have to file bankruptcy to protect your wages from creditors. Look at other alternatives. "Learn before you launch."

A list of the federal bankruptcy exceptions follows. I listed the federal exceptions so you can have an idea of what an exempt property list would look like. For legal reasons, I had to list what states offer the federal exemption as an option. See an experienced bankruptcy attorney in your state on exempt property.

Your state might offer more or less generous exemptions for your personal needs. Consumers of the following states may choose either the federal or their state's exemptions:

States Allowing Choice of Exemptions

Arkansas	Connecticut	District of Columbia	Hawaii
Massachusetts	Michigan	Minnesota	New Jersey
New Mexico	Pennsylvania	Rhode Island	South Carolina
Texas	Vermont	Washington	Wisconsin

Consumers of the states listed below must use their state exemptions only:

States Requiring Use of State Exemptions

Alabama	Alaska	Arizona	Arkansas
California	Colorado	Delaware	Florida
Georgia	Idaho	Indiana	Iowa
Kansas	Kentucky	Louisiana	Maine
Maryland	Mississippi	Missouri	Montana
Nebraska	Nevada	New Hampshire	New York
North Carolina	North Dakota	Ohio	Oklahoma
Oregon	South Dakota	Tennessee	Wyoming
Utah	Virginia	West Virginia	

Federal Bankruptcy Exemptions

Exemptions apply to the equity you have in the property described: for example, the equity you have in your home or automobile. Title 11 U.S.C. Section 522. Married couples double the amount of the federal exemptions that follow.

165

Homestead: Real property, including co-op or mobile home, to $15,000; unused portion of homestead to $7,500 may be applied to any property.

Insurance: Disability, illness or unemployment benefits, life insurance payments for person you depended on, needed for support. Life insurance policy with loan value in accrued dividends or interest to $8,000. Unmatured life insurance contract, except credit insurance policy.

Miscellaneous: Alimony, child support needed for support.

Pensions: ERISA-qualified benefits needed for support.

Personal Property: Animals, crops, clothing, appliances, books, furnishings, household goods, musical instruments to $400 per item, $8,000 total Health Aids, jewelry to $1,000, lost earnings payments, motor vehicle to $2,400, personal injury recoveries to $15,000 (not to include pain and suffering or pecuniary loss), wrongful death recoveries for person you depended on.

Public Benefits: Crime victims' compensation, public assistance Social Security Unemployment compensation, Veterans' benefits.

Tools of Trade: Implements, books & tools of trade to $1,500.

Wages: None.

Wild Card: $800 of any property $7,500 less any amount of homestead exemption claimed of any property.

Non-bankruptcy Exemptions

The following exemptions are available *in addition to* your state's exemptions. They cannot be claimed if you use the federal bankruptcy exemptions.

Retirement: CIA employees, Civil Service employees, Foreign service employees, military honor roll pensions, military service employees, railroad workers, Social Security Veterans' benefits, Veterans' Medal of Honor benefits.

Survivors Benefits: Judges, U.S. Court directors, judicial center directors, supreme court child justice administrators, lighthouse workers, military service.

Death and Disability Benefits: Government employees, longshoremen & harbor workers, war risk hazard, death or injury compensation.

Miscellaneous: Klamath Indians tribe benefits for Indians residing in Oregon Military, deposits in savings accounts while on permanent duty outside the U.S., military group life insurance, railroad workers' unemployment insurance, Seamen's clothing, Seamen's wages (while on a voyage) pursuant to written contract 75% of earned but unpaid wages; bankruptcy judge may authorize more for low-income debtors.

Public Documents

The following pages are public record documents. They are in the public domain and can be used freely. You may reprint or distribute them as much as you want, freely, get them from the web or 800 numbers, even copy them if you wish. Since they were referred to in the book, and for your convenience, they are in this appendix.

Recording
Telephone Conversations

This chapter clarifies policy about recording telephone conversations and includes general information about the interception and divulgence of radio communications.

Recording Interstate or Foreign Telephone Conversations

The FCC protects the privacy of telephone conversations by requiring notification before a recording device is used to record interstate or foreign telephone conversations. These types of conversations may not be recorded unless the use of a recording device is:

- preceded by verbal or written consent of all parties to the telephone conversation or preceded by verbal notification which is recorded at the beginning, and as part of the call, by the recording party;

- or accompanied by an automatic tone warning device, sometimes called a beep tone, which automatically produces a distinct signal that is repeated at regular intervals during the course of the telephone conversation when the recording device is in use.

- Also, no recording device may be used unless it can be physically connected to and disconnected from the telephone line or switched on and off.

The above FCC rule requirements apply to telephone common carriers. Similar requirements are imposed on consumers through the carriers' tariffs. Complaints about Recording Interstate or Foreign Telephone Conversations the FCC's role in assisting consumers who believe their telephone conversations were unlawfully recorded is generally limited to ensuring that telephone companies enforce their tariff provisions regarding recording of telephone conversations. If you believe that someone recorded an interstate or foreign telephone conversation without complying with one of the procedures specified above, you should first contact your local telephone company for assistance. If you are unable to resolve your complaint yourself, you can send a written complaint letter to:

> Federal Communications Commission
> Common Carrier Bureau Consumer Complaints
> Mail Stop Code 1600A2
> Washington, D.C. 20554

Your complaint letter should include the following information: your name, address and a telephone number where you can be reached during the business day; the telephone number involved with your complaint (your home, business or other telephone number where you placed or answered the recorded call); a summary of your complaint, including: the name, address and telephone number of the party who recorded the conversation; the date and time of the recorded conversation; the name of the telephone company you contacted in an effort to resolve your complaint yourself; and the names and telephone numbers of the telephone company employees you spoke with, and the dates you spoke with them.

Recording Intrastate Conversations Questions or complaints about recording intrastate conversations (calls placed within the same state) should be addressed to the state public utility commission for that state. You can contact your local or state consumer office to obtain the telephone number and address for your state public utility commission. This information also may be listed in the government section of your telephone directory.

Interception and Divulgence of Radio Communications there are federal and state laws governing the interception or divulgence of radio communications, including the interception or divulgence of telephone-related radio communications such as cellular or cordless telephone conversations. These laws may make an activity unlawful and may subject the violator to severe criminal penalties. You can browse and download the FCC's Fact Sheet on Interception and Divulgence of Radio Communications from the World Wide Web at

http://www.fcc.gov/Consumer_Info.html#Interception.

You can obtain a copy of this Fact Sheet by calling one the following FCC telephone numbers:

National Call Center, toll-free at 1-888-CALL FCC (1- 888-225-5322). Consumers in some states can reach this toll-free number now.

Office of Public Affairs, Public Service Division, at (202) 418-0200.

Consumer Hotline of the Enforcement Division, Common Carrier Bureau at (202) 632-7553.

Telecommunications Device for the Deaf (TTY) toll-free at 1-888-TELL-FCC (1-888-835-5322).

A Student Loan Borrower's Guide To Defaulted Student Loans

If you are unsure which agency is servicing your defaulted student loan(s), you may call 1-800-4-FED-AID (1-800-433-3243) for an address and telephone number of the agency which holds your defaulted loan(s).

Defaulted Loans Held By a Guaranty Agency. To find out more about your loan held by the guaranty agency serving your state, as well as information about borrowing, please call the Federal Student Aid Information Center at 1-800-4-FED-AID (1-800-433-3243), or check here for a complete list of the guaranty agencies.

Defaulted Loans Held by the U.S. Department of Education. The Department's Debt Collection Service consists of four customer Service Centers located in Washington D.C. (Headquarters), Atlanta (Region IV), Chicago (Region V), and San Francisco (Region IX). You may call Debt Collection Service at (800) 621-3115 for account information regardless of the region your account has been assigned to. Additionally, if your account has been assigned to one of the collection agencies contracted by the Department, you may contact that agency concerning questions related to your account.

U.S. Department of Education
Atlanta Federal Center
19T89 61 Forsyth St. SW
Atlanta, GA 30303

U.S. Department of Education
Chicago Service Center
P.O. Box 8422
Chicago, IL 60680-8422

U.S. Department of Education
San Francisco Service Center
P.O. Box 420410
San Francisco, CA 94142-0410

Fair Debt Collection

August 1996

If you use credit cards, owe money on a personal loan, or are paying on a home mortgage, you are a "debtor." If you fall behind in repaying your creditors, or an error is made on your accounts, you may be contacted by a "debt collector."

You should know that in either situation, the Fair Debt Collection Practices Act requires that debt collectors treat you fairly by prohibiting certain methods of debt collection. Of course, the law does not forgive any legitimate debt you owe.

Commonly asked questions about your rights under the Fair Debt Collection Practices Act follow.

What debts are covered? Personal, family, and household debts are covered under the Act. This includes money owed for the purchase of an automobile, for medical care, or for charge accounts.

Who is a debt collector? A debt collector is any person, other than the creditor who regularly collects debts owed to others. Under a 1986 amendment to the Fair Debt Collection Practices Act, this includes attorneys who collect debts on a regular basis.

How may a debt collector contact you? A collector may contact you in person, by mail, telephone, telegram or fax. However, a debt collector may not contact you at unreasonable times or places, such as before 8 a.m. or after 9 p.m., unless you agree. A debt collector also may not contact you at work if the collector knows that your employer disapproves.

Can you stop a debt collector from contacting you? You can stop a collector from contacting you by writing a letter to the collection agency telling them to stop. Once the agency receives your letter, they may not contact you again except to say there will be no further contact. The agency may notify you if the debt collector or the creditor intends to take some specific action.

Credit and Divorce

January 1998

Mary and Bill recently divorced. Their divorce decree stated that Bill would pay the balances on their three joint credit card accounts. Months later, after Bill neglected to pay off these accounts, all three creditors contacted Mary for payment. She referred them to the divorce decree, insisting that she was not responsible for the accounts. The creditors correctly stated that they were not parties to the decree and that Mary was still legally responsible for paying off the couple's joint accounts. Mary later found out that the late payments appeared on her credit report.

If you've recently been through a divorce—or are contemplating one—you may want to look closely at issues involving credit. Understanding the different kinds of credit accounts opened during a marriage may help illuminate the potential benefits—and pitfalls—of each.

There are two types of credit accounts: individual and joint. You can permit authorized persons to use the account with either. When you apply for credit—whether a charge card or a mortgage loan—you'll be asked to select one type.

Individual or Joint Account

Individual Account: Your income, assets, and credit history are considered by the creditor. Whether you are married or single, you alone are responsible for paying off the debt. The account will appear on your credit report, and may appear on the credit report of any "authorized" user. However, if you live in a community property state (Arizona, California, Idaho, Louisiana, Nevada, New Mexico, Texas, Washington, or Wisconsin), you and your spouse may be responsible for debts incurred during the marriage, and the individual debts of one spouse may appear on the credit report of the other.

Advantages/Disadvantages: If you're not employed outside the home, work part-time, or have a low-paying job, it may be difficult to demonstrate a strong financial picture without your spouse's income. But if you open an account in your name and are responsible, no one can negatively affect your credit record.

Joint Account: Your income, financial assets, and credit history—and your spouse's—are considerations for a joint account. No matter who handles the household bills, you and your spouse are responsible for seeing that debts are paid. A creditor who reports the credit history of a joint account to credit bureaus must report it in both names (if the account was opened after June 1, 1977).

Advantages/Disadvantages: An application combining the financial resources of two people may present a stronger case to a creditor who is granting a loan or credit card. But because two people applied together for the credit, each is responsible for the debt. This is true even if a divorce decree assigns separate debt obligations to each spouse. Former spouses who run up bills and don't pay them can hurt their ex-partner's credit histories on jointly-held accounts.

Account "Users"

If you open an individual account, you may authorize another person to use it. If you name your spouse as the authorized user, a creditor who reports the credit history to a credit bureau must report it in your spouse's name as well as in your's (if the account was opened after June 1, 1977). A creditor also may report the credit history in the name of any other authorized user.

Advantages/Disadvantages: User accounts often are opened for convenience. They benefit people who might not qualify for credit on their own, such as students or homemakers. While these people may use the account, you—not they—are contractually liable for paying the debt.

If You Divorce

If you're considering divorce or separation, pay special attention to the status of your credit accounts. If you maintain joint accounts during this time, it's important to make regular payments so your credit record won't suffer. As long as there's an outstanding balance on a joint account, you and your spouse are responsible for it.

If you divorce, you may want to close joint accounts or accounts in which your former spouse was an authorized user. Or ask the creditor to convert these accounts to individual accounts. By law, a creditor cannot close a joint account because of a change in marital status, but can do so at the request of either spouse. A creditor, however, does not have to change joint accounts to individual accounts. The creditor can require you to reapply for credit on an individual basis and then, based on your new application, extend or deny you credit. In the case of a mortgage or home equity loan, a lender is likely to require refinancing to remove a spouse from the obligation.

For More Information

The FTC publishes a series of free consumer brochures on credit issues. You also can request a free copy of Best Sellers, a complete list of FTC publications, at:

Consumer Response Center
Federal Trade Commission
Washington, D.C. 20580

(202) 326-2222.

TDD: (202) 326-2502.

May a debt collector contact anyone else about your debt? If you have an attorney, the debt collector may not contact anyone other than your attorney. If you do not have an attorney, a collector may contact other people, but only to find out where you live and work. Collectors usually are prohibited from contacting such permissible third parties more than once. In most cases, the collector may not tell anyone other than you and your attorney that you owe money.

What must the debt collector tell you about the debt? Within five days after you are first contacted, the collector must send you a written notice telling you the amount of money you owe; the name of the creditor to whom you owe the money; and what action to take if you believe you do not owe the money.

May a debt collector continue to contact you if you believe you do not owe money? A collector may not contact you if, within 30 days after you are first contacted, you send the collection agency a letter stating you do not owe money. However, a collector can renew collection activities if you are sent proof of the debt, such as a copy of a bill for the amount owed.

What types of debt collection practices are prohibited? Harassment. Debt collectors may not harass, oppress or abuse anyone. For example, debt collectors may not:

- use threats of violence or harm against the person, property, or reputation;
- publish a list of consumers who refuse to pay their debts (except to a credit bureau);
- use obscene or profane language;
- repeatedly use the telephone to annoy someone;
- telephone people without identifying themselves;
- advertise your debt.

False statements. Debt collectors may not use any false statements when collecting a debt. For example, debt collectors may not:

- falsely imply that they are attorneys or government representatives;
- falsely imply that you have committed a crime;
- falsely represent that they operate or work for a credit

bureau;

- misrepresent the amount of your debt;
- misrepresent the involvement of an attorney in collecting a debt;
- indicate that papers being sent to you are legal forms when they are not;
- indicate that papers being sent to you are not legal forms when they are.

Debt collectors also may not state that:

You will be arrested if you do not pay your debt; they will seize, garnish, attach, or sell your property or wages, unless the collection agency or creditor intends to do so, and it is legal to do so; actions, such as a lawsuit, will be taken against you, which legally may not be taken, or which they do not intend to take.

Debt collectors may not:

Give false credit information about you to anyone; send you anything that looks like an official document from a court or government agency when it is not; use a false name.

Unfair practices.

Debt collectors may not engage in unfair practices when they try to collect a debt. For example, collectors may not:

Collect any amount greater than your debt, unless allowed by law; deposit a postdated check prematurely; make you accept collect calls or pay for telegrams; take or threaten to take your property unless this can be done legally; contact you by postcard.

What control do you have over payment of debts? If you owe more than one debt, any payment you make must be applied to the debt you indicate. A debt collector may not apply a payment to any debt you believe you do not owe.

What can you do if you believe a debt collector violated the law? You have the right to sue a collector in a state or federal court within one year from the date you believe the law was violated. If you win, you may recover money for the damages you suffered. Court costs and attorneys fees also can be recovered. A group of people also may sue a debt collector and recover money for damages up to $500,000, or one percent of the collectors net worth, whichever is less.

Where can you report a debt collector for an alleged violation? Report any problems you have with a debt collector to your state Attorney Generals office and the Federal Trade Commission. Many states have their own debt collection laws and your Attorney Generals office can help you determine your rights.

If you have questions about the Fair Debt Collection Practices Act, or your rights under the Act, write:

> Correspondence Branch
> Federal Trade Commission
> Washington, D.C. 20580.

Although the FTC generally cannot intervene in individual disputes, the information you provide may indicate a pattern of possible law violations requiring action by the Commission.

To obtain a free copy of Best Sellers, a list of all the FTC's consumer and business publications, contact:

> Consumer Repsonse Center
> Federal Trade Commission
> Washington, D.C. 20580.
> 202-326-2222.
> TDD: 202-326-2502

State Attorneys General Addresses And Phone Numbers

These are the most recent phone numbers.

Alabama Consumer Protection Division
Office of Attorney General
11 S. Union St. Montgomery, AL 36130
334-242-7300
800-392- 5658
Fax 334-242-7458.

Alaska Attorney General
P. O. Box K
Juneau, AK 99811-0300
907- 465-3600
Fax 907-465-2075.

Arizona Consumer Protection Division
Office of Attorney General
1275 W. Washington St., Room 259
Phoenix, AZ 85007
602-542-3702
800-352-8431
Fax 602-542-4085.

Arkansas Consumer Protection Division
Office of Attorney General
200 Tower Building
4th & 323 Center St.
Little Rock, AR 72201
501-682- 2341
800-482-8982
Fax 501-682-8084.

California Public Inquiry Unit
Office of Attorney General
1515 K St., Suite 511

or P.O. Box 944255
Sacramento, CA 94244-2550
916-322- 3360
800-952-5225

California Department of Consumer Affairs
1020 N St.
Sacramento, CA 95814
916-445-0660
800-344-9940
Fax 916-324-4298.

Colorado Consumer Protection Unit
Office of Attorney General
1525 Sherman Street
Denver, CO 80203
303-866-5189
800-332-2071
Fax 303-866-5691.

Connecticut Department of Consumer Protection
165 Capital Ave.
Hartford, CT 06106
860-566-2816
Fax 860-566-1531.

Delaware Division of Consumer Affairs
Department of Community Affairs
820 N. French St., 4th Floor
Wilmington, DE 19801
302-577-3250
Fax 302-577-2610.

District of Columbia
Department of Consumer and Regulatory Affairs
614 H St., NW Room 1120
Washington, DC 20001
202-727-7170
Fax 202-727-8073.

Florida Division of Consumer Services
235 Mayo Building
Tallahassee, FL 32399-0800
904-488-2226

800-327-3382
Fax 904- 488-0863.

Georgia Office of Consumer Affairs
40 Capitol Square
Atlanta, GA 30334-1300
404-656-3383
Fax 404-651-9148.

Hawaii Office of Consumer Protection
Department of Commerce and Consumer Affairs
828 Fort Street Mall
or P.O. Box 3767
Honolulu, HI 96813-3767
808-586-2630
Fax 808 586-2640.

Idaho Consumer Protection Division
Office of the Attorney General
700 West Jefferson Street
P. O. Box 83720
Boise, ID 83720-0010
208-334-2424
800-432-3545
Fax 208-334-2530.

Illinois Governor's Office of Citizens Assistance
222 South College
401 FLR
Springfield, IL 62706
217-782-0244
800-642-3112.

Indiana Consumer Protection Division
Office of Attorney General
219 State House
Indianapolis, IN 46204
317-232-6330
800-382-5516.

Iowa Citizens' Aide
215 E. 7th St.
Capitol Complex
Des Moines, IA 50319

515-281-3592
800-358-5510.

Kansas Consumer Protection Division
Office of Attorney General
Kansas Judicial Center
301 West 10th St.
Topeka, KS 66612
913-296- 3751
800-432-2310.

Kentucky Consumer Protection Division
Office of Attorney General
209 St. Clair St.
Frankfort, KY 40601
502-564-2200
800-432-9257.

Louisiana Consumer Protection Section
Office of Attorney General
State Capitol Building
P.O. Box 94005
Baton Rouge, LA 70804
504-342-7013
Fax 504-342-7901.

Maine Bureau of Consumer Credit Protection
State House Station # 35
Augusta, ME 04333-0035
207-624-8527
800-332-8529
Fax 207-624-8690.

Maryland Consumer Protection Division
Office of Attorney General
200 St. Paul Plc.
Baltimore, MD 21202-2022
410-476-6550
Fax 410-576-7003.

Massachusetts Consumer Protection Division
Department of Attorney General
131 Tremont St.

Boston, MA 02111
617-727-7780.

Michigan Consumer Protection Division
Office of Attorney General
P.O. Box 30213
Lansing, MI 48909
517-335-0855
Fax 517-373-4916.

Minnesota Office of Consumer Services
Office of Attorney General
Rm. 124, Ford Bldg.
117 University Ave.
St. Paul, MN 55155
612-296-2331.

Mississippi Consumer Protection Division
Office of Attorney General
P.O. Box 220
Jackson, MS 39205
601-359-4230
Fax 601-359-3441.

Missouri Public Protection Division
Office of Attorney General
P.O. Box 899
Jefferson City, MO 65102
314-751-3321
800-392-8222
Fax 314-751-0774.

Montana Office of Consumer Affairs
Department of Commerce
1424 9th Ave.
Helena, MT 59620
406-444-4312
406-444-3553
Fax 406-444-2903.

Nebraska Consumer Protection Division
Department of Justice
2115 State Capitol Room 2115
Lincoln, NE 68509

402-471-4723
402-471-2682
Fax 402-471-3297.

Nevada Consumer Affairs Division
Department of Commerce
4600 Kietezke Ln, Bldg. M., Ste. 245
Reno, NV 89502
702-688-1800
800-992-0900.

New Hampshire Office of the Attorney
General Consumer Protection
33 Capitol Street
Concord NH 03301
603-271-3641
Fax 603-271-2110.

New Jersey Division of Consumers Affairs
P. O. Box 45025
Newark, NJ 07101
973-504-6200
Fax 973-648-3538.

New Mexico Consumer and Economic Crime Division
Office of Attorney General
P.O. Drawer 1508
Santa Fe, NM 87504
505-827-6060
800-432-2070.

New York Consumer Protection
99 Washington Ave.
Albany, NY 12210
518-474-8583
Fax 518-474-2474.

New York Bureau of Consumer Frauds and Protection
Office of Attorney General
The Capitol Albany, NY 12224
518-474-5481.

North Carolina Consumer Protection Division
Office of Attorney General
P.O. Box 629
Raleigh, NC 27602
919-716-6000.

North Dakota Consumer Fraud Division
Office of Attorney General
600 East. Blvd.
Bismarck, ND 58505
701-328-3404
800-472-2600.

Ohio Consumer Frauds and Crimes Section
Office of Attorney General
30 E. Broad St.
State Office Tower, 25th Floor
Columbus, OH 43266-0410
614-466-4986
800-282-0515
Fax 614-466-5087.

Oklahoma Consumer Office of Attorney General
112 State Capitol Building
Oklahoma City, OK 73105
405-521-4274
Fax 405-521-6246.

Oregon Financial Fraud Section
Consumer Complaints
Department of Justice
Justice Building, Salem, OR 97310
503-378-4320
Fax 503-378-3784.

Pennsylvania Bureau of Consumer Protection
Office of Attorney General
Strawberry Square, 14th Floor
Harrisburg, PA 17120
717-787- 9707
800-441-2555
Fax 717-787-1190.

Puerto Rico Department of Consumer Affairs Minil-
las Station P.O. Box 41059
Santurce, PR 00940
809-722-7555.

Rhode Island Consumer Protection Division
Department of Attorney General
72 Pine St. Providence, RI 02903
401-222-2104
800-852-7776.

South Carolina Department of Consumer Affairs
P.O. Box 5757
Columbia, SC 29250
803-734-9452
800-922-1594
Fax 803-734-9365.

South Dakota Division of Consumer Affairs
Office of Attorney General
500 East Capitol, Capitol Building
Pierre, SD 57501
605-773-4400
Fax 605-773-4106.

Tennessee Division of Consumer Affairs
500 James Robertson Parkway, 5th Floor
Nashville, TN 37243-0600
615-741-4737
800-342-8385.

Texas Consumer Protection Division
Office of Attorney General
Capitol Station
P.O. Box 12548
Austin, TX 78711
512-463-2100
512-463-2070
Fax 512-463-2063.

Utah Division of Consumer Protection
Department of Commerce
160 E. 3rd South
P.O. Box 45802

Salt Lake City, UT 84145-0802
801-530-6601
Fax 801-530-6001.

Vermont Public Protection Division
Office of Attorney General
109 State St.
Montpelier, VT 05609
802-828-3171
800-649-2424
Fax 802-828-2154.

Virgin Islands Department of Licensing and Consumer Affairs Property and Procurement Building
Subbase #1, Room 205
St. Thomas, VI 00802
809-774-3130.

Virginia Division of Consumer Affairs
P.O. Box 1163
Richmond, VA 23209
804-786-2042
800-552-9963
Fax 804-371-2945.

Washington Consumer and Business Fair Practice
Division
Office of Attorney General
900 4th Ave., Ste. 2000
Seattle, WA 98164
360-733-6200
800-551-4636
Fax 360-664-0228.

West Virginia Consumer Protection Division
Attorney General
1900 Kanawha Blvd. E. # 1
Charleston, WS 25305
304-558-8986
800-368-8808
Fax 304-5880104.

Wisconsin Consumer Protection Agency
123 West Washington Ave. Room 150
Madison, WI 53707
608-266-1852
800-425-3328
Fax 608-267-2223.

Wyoming Consumers Affairs Division
Office of Attorney General
123 State Capital Building
Cheyenne, WY 82002
307-777-7891
Fax 307-777-6869.

Federal Trade Commission Offices

Federal Trade Commission Headquarters.

Send your questions or complaints to:

Consumer Response Center
Federal Trade Commission
6th Street & Pennsylvania Ave., NW
Washington, DC 20580
202-326-2222 or www.ftc.gov
TDD: 202-326-2502.

Regional Offices:

Atlanta Regional Office Federal Trade Commission

Suite 5M
3560 Forsyth Street, SW
Atlanta, GA 30303-2322.

For Consumer Complaint Calls: 404-656-1399
Business Calls: 404-656-1390. Fax: 404-656-1379.

Atlanta Regional Office serves the residents of the following states:
Alabama, Florida, Georgia, Mississippi, North Carolina, South Carolina, Tennessee, and Virginia.

Boston Regional Office Federal Trade Commission

101 Merrimac Street
Suite 810
Boston, MA 02114-4719.

For Consumer Complaint Calls: 617-424-5960.
Business Calls: 617-424-5960. Fax: 617-424-5998.

Boston Regional Office serves the residents of the following states:
Connecticut, Maine, Massachusetts, New Hampshire, Rhode Island, and Vermont. Chicago Regional Office Federal Trade Commission

55 East Monroe Street, Suite 1860
Chicago, IL 60603-5701.

For Consumer Complaint Calls: 312-960-5633. Fax: 312-960-5600.

Chicago Regional Office serves the residents of the following states:

Illinois, Indiana, Iowa, Kentucky, Minnesota, Missouri, and Wisconsin.

Cleveland Regional Office Federal Trade Commission

1111 Superior Avenue, Suite 200
Cleveland, OH 44114-2507.

For Consumer Complaint Calls: 216-263-3410. Fax: 216-263-3426.

Cleveland Regional Office serves the residents of the following states:

Delaware, District of Columbia, Maryland, Michigan, Ohio, Pennsylvania, and West Virginia.

Dallas Regional Office Federal Trade Commission

1999 Bryan Street, Suite 2150
Dallas, TX 75201-6808.

For Consumer Complaint Calls: 214-979-0213.
This number is answered between 8:30 a.m. and 12 Noon, Monday through Friday.

Dallas Regional Office serves the residents of the following states:

Arkansas, Louisiana, New Mexico, Oklahoma, and Texas.

Denver Regional Office Federal Trade Commission

1961 Stout Street, Suite 1523
Denver, CO 80294-0101.

For Consumer Complaint Calls: 303-844-2271.

Denver Regional Office serves the residents of the following states:

Colorado, Kansas, Montana, Nebraska, North Dakota, South Dakota, Utah, and Wyoming.

Arizona and Southern California.

Federal Trade Commission
Los Angeles Regional Office
10877 Wilshire Blvd., Suite 700
Los Angeles, California 90024.

For Consumer Complaint Calls: 310-824-4300.

Northern California, Hawaii, and Nevada.

San Francisco Regional Office Federal Trade Commission
901 Market Street, Suite 570
San Francisco, CA 94103.

For Consumer Complaint Calls: 415-356-5270.

Business Calls: 415-356-5270. Fax: 415-356-5284.

New Jersey and New York.

Federal Trade Commission
150 William Street, Suite 1300
New York, NY 10038.

For Consumer Complaint Calls: 212-264-1207.

Business Calls: 212-264-1207. Fax: 212-264-0459.

Alaska, Idaho, Oregon, and Washington.

Seattle Regional Office Federal Trade Commission
2806 Federal Building, 915 Second Ave.
Seattle, WA 98174.

For Consumer Complaint Calls: 206-220-6363.

Business Calls: 206-220-6350. Fax: 206-220-6366

Index

"Among all the debt and broken contracts, it's still a beautiful country, so be gentle on yourself."

Good luck on the future of your personal finances.

Your input is important to me. Write to me at the address below. If your library doesn't have this book, please ask them to get it for other readers. If your local book store does not carry *Debt Control*, order it toll-free (888) 340-3328 or mail check or money order for $19.95 plus $3 for shipping to:

Debt Control
P. O. Box 58451
Houston, TX 77058.

Please visit the author's website:
http://www.debtcontrol.com.